THE CROSS AND
THE RAIN FOREST

A Critique of Radical Green Spirituality

THE CROSS AND THE RAIN FOREST

A Critique of Radical Green Spirituality

Robert Whelan, Joseph Kirwan
and Paul Haffner

ACTON INSTITUTE FOR THE STUDY OF RELIGION AND LIBERTY

WILLIAM B. EERDMANS PUBLISHING COMPANY

Copyright © 1996 by the
ACTON INSTITUTE
FOR THE STUDY OF RELIGION AND LIBERTY

Published jointly 1996 by the
Acton Institute for the Study of Religion and Liberty
161 Ottawa Avenue, NW, Suite 301
Grand Rapids, Michigan 49503
Phone: (616) 454-3080   Fax: (616) 454-9454
and by
Wm. B. Eerdmans Publishing Co.
255 Jefferson Ave. S.E., Grand Rapids, Michigan 49503

Printed in the United States of America

00 99 98 97 96   5 4 3 2 1

Library of Congress Cataloging-in-Publication Data

Whelan, Robert.
The Cross and the rain forest: a critique of radical green spirituality /
Robert Whelan, Joseph Kirwan, Paul Haffner.
p.   cm.
Includes bibliographical references and index.
Eerdmans ISBN 0-8028-4201-1 (alk. paper)
Acton Institute ISBN 1-880595-07-9 (alk. paper)
1. Human ecology — Religious aspects — Christianity. 2. Theology,
Doctrinal.   I. Kirwan, Joseph.   II. Haffner, Paul, 1954-   .   III. Title.
BT695.5.W54   1996
261.8′362 — dc20   96- 21209
                                    CIP

Scriptural quotations are taken from the Jerusalem Bible, first published in the
UK by Dartman, Longman and Todd Ltd and in the USA by Doubleday and
Company Inc. in 1966, with the exception of the Psalms, which are taken from
the Grail version, first published in the UK by Collins in Fontana Books, 1963.

Contents

ACKNOWLEDGEMENTS

My thanks are due to Alejandro Chafuen, President of the Atlas Economic Research Foundation in Fairfax, Virginia, his Board and his staff, especially Jo Kwong, for their assistance and support. Without the opportunities which were provided by my Atlas Summer Fellowship I doubt if the project could have been brought to completion. Thanks also to Roger Nesbitt and members of the Faith Movement in the UK, who introduced me to the work of Stanley Jaki, which is crucial to any understanding of the issues discussed here. Finally, all those who labour in this particular vineyard owe an immeasurable debt to the work of Julian Simon. He sets the standards by which we must be judged.

RW

(St) Boniface ... made a bold attempt to strike at the root of the pagan super-stitions which constituted the chief hindrance to the progress of the Gospel as well as to the stability of recent converts. On a day which had been pub-licly announced, and in the midst of an awestruck crowd, he attacked with an axe one of the chief objects of popular veneration, Donar's sacred oak, which stood on the summit of Mount Gudenberg at Geismar, near Fritzlar. Almost as the first blows fell upon it, the huge tree crashed, splitting into four parts, and the people who had expected a judgement to descend upon the perpetra-tors of such an outrage acknowledged that their gods were powerless to pro-tect their own sanctuaries. From that time the work of evangelization ad-vanced steadily.

From *Butler's Lives of the Saints: St Boniface*

I seek a god, old tree: accept my worship, thou!
All other gods have failed me always in my need.
I hang my votive song beneath thy temple bough,
Unto thy strength I cry — Old monster, be my creed!

Richard Le Gallienne, *Tree-Worship*, 1894

Foreword

The distinctive trait of popular theology is its transparent trendiness. A few years ago, the cause was socialism in the guise of liberation theology. Before that it was the interventionist state in the form of the social gospel. Who can be surprised that now many religious spokesmen have baptized secular environmentalism and proclaimed it as the newest *good news*?

Would that we could dismiss this trend as an aberration, to be forgotten next year and replaced with the next excuse for avoiding the rigors of orthodoxy. But, through hard experience, we have learned that the religious version of secular statism can be damaging indeed — both to society and to the integrity of the faith.

The new green faith poses a threat to orthodox religion and its view of the relationship between God and the created order, as these insightful essays make clear. In its many manifestations eco-religion proposes a new god to take the place of the Creator in the religious tradition of Christendom. And misguided Christians have been backing away from the central articles of faith that environmentalists have attacked as harmful to the earth.

So that we are clear about orthodoxy, let us turn to St. Ignatius of Loyola:

> Man is created to praise, reverence, and serve God our Lord, and by this means to save his soul. The other things on the face of the earth are created for man to help him in attaining the end for which he is created. Hence, man is to make use of them in as far as they help him in the attainment of his end ...

Contrast this view with secular environmentalist ideology. Many environmentalists have tried to invert the hierarchy of the created order, making the human person absolutely subordinate to the rest. By graft-

ix

ing this view onto faith, we superimpose an exaggerated view of the non-human creation above God's primary creation.

In some cases, worshipping the earth, instead of our Lord, becomes the essence of the faith. In other cases, religious values are merely confused, as environmentalist causes are emphasized at the expense of sound doctrine. Both views fit well within the context of the radical environmentalist agenda.

There is, of course, a place for nature in a theologically formed civic life, as Paul Haffner explains herein. St. Francis was known for his love of animals, but not in the same way he loved other people, created in God's image. St. Francis believed that all of God's creation is worthy of our respect by virtue of the Author. Indeed, he even believed in the hierarchy among the animals.

The scholastic view of creation similarly regards man as the noblest part of creation. He has a soul, which separates him from the rest of creation. Humans have transcendent life, where the animals have only a temporal existence. In the Genesis account, God commanded man to mix his labor with creation to make more of it than what appears to us in the state of nature. God's covenant with Adam requires him to exercise dominion over the earth, His gift to us for our use. We cannot keep man from his surroundings, from nature, from the environment. Nature does not have a metaphysical right to be left alone, to be preserved and adored for reasons other than its usefulness to God's human creation.

This is what environmentalists find so objectionable. At God's command, man uses his environment for human betterment and for the attainment of salvation. In contrast, the goal of modern environmentalism is to diminish the extent to which people can have an effect — even if it results in something more pleasing — on the original state of nature. God's command to till and keep the soil is transformed into state regulations, centrally enforced.

Secular liberalism, having successfully banished orthodox religion from public life, is now eager to use heterodox spirituality for its own purposes. Environmental indoctrination in the public schools is a prime example. While the crucifix is banned from the classroom, children are taught pagan beliefs about the sacredness of the environment and the 'circle of life' which we share with the animals. Teaching children to worship Mother Nature through song and activities is acceptable, though the Bible cannot even be used as an historical text.

This series of outstanding essays provides the necessary corrective. People of all orthodox faiths will find it of great service in identifying the ancient and modern confusion of the eco-religion. As with all political distortions of the faith, we do well to remember that the goal of life is salvation through faith and the avoidance of sin. To avoid sin, we must obey God's law. His first commandment to us is to have no false gods before Him, even when the new god is, once again, being advanced by élite opinion.

Fr. Robert A. Sirico
The Acton Institute
Grand Rapids, Michigan
May 1996

INTRODUCTION
The Healing Power of Cardboard

Robert Whelan

Annihilating all that's made
To a green Thought in a green Shade
'The Garden' by Andrew Marvell (1621-78)

The marriage between Christianity and the Green movement has been loudly proclaimed and widely celebrated, if the number of books on the subject to be found in religious bookshops is any guide.

For many Christians today, the mission to save the earth is *the* important ministry. The alleviation of poverty is no longer at the top of the list of social priorities, and missionary activity, as traditionally understood, seems to be regarded by some as an embarrassment.

Tim Cooper's *Green Christianity* and Sean McDonagh's *The Greening of the Church*, both bestsellers in Christian terms, illustrate the extent to which the very mission of the church on earth has been tinted green. Here are some of the examples given of ways in which modern Christians can fulfil Christ's command to be the salt of the earth and the light of the world:

> * Missionaries have ... been active as naturalists and many have done valuable work to improve the lives of the poor. Many of them have unique opportunities to help solve environmental problems as they work in tropical forest regions.[1]

> * Has the church considered campaigning against sources of pollution such as power station emissions and vehicles?[2]

> * The elimination of bird life is an ecological and spiritual disaster. The Church should combat this by systematic moral teaching about

1

biocide (the destruction of species) and by bird liturgies which energize the human spirit.[3]

* In 1986 the group [Community Recycling Opportunities Programme] recycled 1,200 tonnes of material waste ... Robert Browne said that he felt that it was a very important religious work given the crisis which our planet now faces. He feels that it is time that the Church moved with force into this area. He says that he can testify to 'the healing power of cardboard'.[4]

Is this really the best way in which Christians can respond to the needs of the modern world? Can the Christian's obligation of mission be discharged within the narrow compass of bird liturgies and 'the healing power of cardboard'?

In his book *Greenhouse Theology* Ron Elsdon tells the story of the A Rocha project in Portugal, through which a house in the Algarve was purchased and fitted out as a study centre for bird, insect, and plant life under two wardens, Peter and Miranda Harris.

Surprisingly perhaps, the Harrises have been seconded to the project by BCMS Crosslinks, an evangelical Anglican mission agency. When the Harrises first applied to this agency for Christian service overseas, East Africa seemed the most likely destination for them. When the time came, however, no suitable place was available for them there. What followed was a clear demonstration of God's guidance. The Harris and Batty families, on holiday together, had a shared vision of a Christian Bird Observatory, and were so convinced by the strength of it that the Harrises no longer believed East Africa was the right destination for them. Meanwhile BCMS Crosslinks was revising its statement of faith, and believed on scriptural grounds that mission includes the care of creation. It was from these two sets of circumstances that the Harrises were seconded to the A Rocha project. [5]

When birdwatching in the Algarve is regarded as a reasonable alternative to spreading the Good News of Jesus Christ in Africa, it is clear that the church's understanding of mission is undergoing a radical change.

Ron Elsdon admits that 'the evangelistic impact of A Rocha is hard to quantify' (presumably because there is as yet no rite of baptism for birds) but goes on to say that:

> One of the visions of the A Rocha Project is that it will help others to catch visions of exciting new ways of declaring the good news in all its fullness.[6]

Sean McDonagh, an Irish Columban missionary, would seem to agree:

> Gradually it is beginning to dawn on many people that alleviating poverty, healing nature and preserving the stability of the biosphere is the central task for those who follow in the footsteps of Jesus in today's world.[7]

Only the first of these three aims is directly involved with the welfare of human beings. More importantly, evangelisation, in the traditional sense of winning converts to Christianity, does not figure on the list.

Altered Priorities

The mildest criticism which could be made of Green Christianity is that it appears to involve a radical re-ordering of priorities. For example, the Movement for Christian Democracy published a list of things which are 'badly wrong in Britain', which put in first place the destruction of '97% of wildflower meadows and 190,000 miles of hedgerow'. The fact that one pregnancy in five is terminated by abortion comes fourth.[8]

Its defenders would claim that this re-ordering of priorities is necessary in view of the fact that we have brought the whole natural world to the point of collapse by our plundering of nature. If we don't change our ways, they argue, there will be no future generations of Christians or non-Christians.

However, critics of the movement warn that by embracing the Green agenda so enthusiastically some Christians, including church leaders, have associated themselves with a movement which is essentially hostile to the values of the Judaeo-Christian tradition, and which may even be closer to paganism.

Tim Cooper believes that:

> ... the appalling plight of the environment is leading many Christians

3

to reconsider the place of humankind in relation to the rest of nature.[9]

However, this reconsideration may involve more profound theological ramifications than Cooper realises. 'The place of humankind' in relation to the natural order has been defined, for Christians, by the Book of Genesis. The cosmology which we learn from Genesis — which means the explanation offered by Christianity for the origin and creation of the universe — is one of the most profound of Christian doctrines. The relationship of man to nature is derived from that cosmology. Any attempt to redefine our position, or to 'resacralise our relationship with the planet'[10] as American author Jeremy Rifkin puts it, runs the risk of transforming Christianity into something different.

Two stories, both of which concern the involvement in African affairs by well-meaning Europeans, may be used to illustrate the practical consequences of this shifting view of the importance of human beings in the natural order.

Mary Tiffen, Michael Mortimore and Francis Gichuki have written a detailed account of the development of the Machakos district in Kenya entitled *More People, Less Erosion*. This reveals that, at the end of the last century, the area was almost completely unpopulated owing to the dangers posed by wild animals. In 1896 a Christian mission station was set up and the missionaries set about shooting the animals. As a result families moved into the area to farm.[11] It is highly unlikely that modern missionaries would see it as part of their ministry to shoot wildlife: they would be far more likely to be in the vanguard of movements to preserve it!

In September 1990 the World Wide Fund for Nature (WWF) found itself involved in controversy when it was revealed that a helicopter had been provided by the charity to stop poaching of the black rhino in Zimbabwe, even though the government had a shoot to kill policy. 37 poachers had been shot in Zimbabwe between 1987-8. WWF Director George Medley defended the decision, saying that the helicopter had been provided on the 'strict understanding it would never be used as a gunship.'[12]

The Need for Balance

None of the contributors to this volume believes that care for the environment is either a trivial or worthless pursuit. Of course we all want to have a good environment. Nobody wants to breathe polluted air or to drink poisoned water.

However we feel it is necessary to warn Christians of the pitfalls which can ensue from embracing the Green movement, as it is currently constituted, too warmly. At the heart of Greenery lie values which are fundamentally different from those of our Judaeo-Christian tradition. In a famous article published in Science in 1967 American historian Lynn White blamed Christianity for environmental degradation, and warned that we would have to 'find a new religion, or rethink our old one' if we wanted to undo the damage.[13] Some Christians are concerned that the rethinking of Christianity which has gone on in recent years with regard to Green issues has come close to creating Lynn White's new religion.

In 1989 Fr. Giovanni Moletta, a professor of moral theology in the seminary of Vicenza, told a conference of environmentalists that he had refused absolution to a factory manager who was guilty of polluting the environment. He was supported in his stance by the Bishop of Vicenza who called for an 11th commandment forbidding pollution, which he wanted to be put on a par with murder.[14] We need to be quite clear that neither scripture nor tradition provides the scope for Bishops or anyone else to make up new commandments. God gave Moses enough of them, for the Jews and for us.

If we are to stop the transformation, or dilution, of the authentic Christian message, we must at least be aware of the origins and implications of Greenery. The contributors to this short volume of essays have looked at Green attitudes towards God, towards human beings, towards animals and towards the science of ecology. Their findings would seem to suggest that the conflicting world-views of Christianity and Greenery may prove irreconcilable, unless the former is to be totally subsumed by the latter.

NOTES

1. Tim Cooper,*Green Christianity*, London: Spire (1990) p. 184.
2. Ibid., p. 254.

3. Sean McDonagh, *The Greening of the Church*, London: Geoffrey Chapman (1990) p. 96.
4. Ibid., p. 200.
5. Ron Elsdon, *Greenhouse Theology*, Tunbridge Wells: Monarch Publications (1992) p. 194.
6. Ibid., pp. 194 and 195.
7. Sean McDonagh, op.cit., p. 163-4.
8. Membership leaflet *Movement for Christian Democracy: A Christian Initiative in British Politics* (undated).
9. Tim Cooper, op.cit., p. 41.
10. Jeremy Rifkin, *Biosphere Politics: A New Consciousness for a New Century*, New York: Crown Publishers Inc. (1991) p. 48.
11. Mary Tiffen, Michael Mortimore and Francis Gichuki, *More People, Less Erosion; Environmental Recovery in Kenya*, Chichester: John Wiley and Sons (1993) p. 44.
12. Kate Parkin, 'Nature group in cash links with arms giants', *The Daily Express* (5 September 1990).
13. Lynn White Jr, 'The Historical Roots of our Ecologic Crisis', *Science* (10 March 1967) Vol.155, No 3767, p. 1206
14. *The Daily Telegraph* (13 May 1989).

CHAPTER ONE

Greens and God

Robert Whelan

Everything to be true must become a religion. And agnosticism should have its ritual no less than faith.
                                    Oscar Wilde, *De Profundis,* 1897

Members of the various Green Parties in Europe sometimes claim that theirs is the first political movement which is based on science, instead of on the old divisions of right and left. This claim is not original, however. Marx and Engels invoked the scientific principle in defence of their economic theories, but perhaps the most persistent political aspirants to the mantle of science were the Nazis. They claimed that Nazism simply represented the putting into effect of the findings of the 'science' of eugenics, or racial hygiene. This 'science' had been developed from the end of the nineteenth century to explain all human behaviour and characteristics in terms of genetic inheritance. It taught that people either have good genes (eugenic) or bad genes (dysgenic) and that nothing can be done about it—apart from stopping the dysgenic ones from reproducing and weakening the racial stock. No other possible explanation for behaviour, such as education, environmental factors or religious belief, was countenanced. The pure blood line was everything.

The Nazis clung to their 'science' as the justification for everything that happened. Rudolf Hess used to say that Nazism was just 'applied biology', and of course the most characteristic horror of Nazism, which will be remembered until the end of time, was the abuse of science which occurred in the concentration camps where human beings were treated as laboratory animals in experiments which infected them with disease and inflicted death in a variety of pitiless ways.

How could the scientists have done it? How did it arise that men who, in other circumstances, might have been effective doctors or laboratory technicians, came to stitch together human subjects, or drown them, or crush them in pursuit of scientific data?

Nazis and the Environment

In view of the current craze for Greenery, the Nazi attitude towards the environment is also of interest. In many ways Nazism was a very Green creed. It placed great emphasis on the strong, dark forests and the pure streams of the Fatherland as a source of strength. Nazi Germany was the first European nation to create nature reserves and to decree that all forest plantations had to include broad-leafed deciduous trees together with conifers.[1] As soon as the Nazis gained power in 1933 they began legislating to protect rare species, and on 17 August 1933 Hermann Göring issued orders that 'persons who engage in vivisection of any kind will be deported to concentration camps'.[2] There was great interest in holistic medicine and vegetarianism, Hitler himself being a non-smoking, non-drinking vegetarian.[3]

When people try to trace the political and philosophical antecedents of the present Green movement, Nazism is the bit they leave out, for obvious reasons. The purpose of this comparison is not to suggest that all vegetarians are Nazis, or that tree planting is indicative of the mindset of the Master Race, but to draw attention to the much more important and fundamental similarity between Nazism and the Green movement: the attitude towards science.

Junk Science

The important thing about Nazi science is that it was junk science. No one now takes racial hygiene seriously. It represented the mixture of a few facts with a great deal of bigotry and racial prejudice. Similarly, much of what passes for science amongst the Greens would more properly be described as junk science or pseudo-science. It represents the same heady mixture of a few facts with much pressure-group politics, all garbed in the striking purple prose of the apocalypse.

For example, Al Gore tells us that 'we are now engaged in an epic battle to right the balance of our earth', and he is unable to discuss the effect of CFCs on the ozone layer without thundering: 'Ultimately, it's about the entire relationship between human civilization and the global environment'.[4] Heady stuff, but not good science.

It will probably come as a surprise to most readers to learn that there is no scientific consensus — and in some cases no compelling evidence — which supports even the key scare stories in the arch of the environmental holocaust. There is no 'hole' in the ozone layer, no evidence that current levels of ozone are unusually thin, and no increase in ultra-violet rays reaching the earth; species are not known to be disappearing at an alarming rate—in fact it is difficult to be sure that any are disappearing at all; loss of the tropical rain forests is proceeding at a rate of less than one per cent a year, with absolutely no possibility of wiping the rain forests off the face of the earth in the foreseeable future; and, most importantly, global warming, that mother of all environmental scares, is a myth. The global climate shows no trend towards catastrophic warming and, in any case, the extent to which human activities could affect climate is probably negligible. (Readers who find these claims incredible or perverse should turn to the Appendix: Science Facts which summarises the scientific evidence.)

Claiming that 'science' has shown that man has polluted the environment to the point of ecological collapse, some Greens are demanding a response which would actually alter the very nature of human societies. 'The human future is at risk', according to the Eminent Persons group which met in Tokyo prior to the 1992 Earth Summit. 'It is time to re-evaluate the thinking which underlies our present society'.[5] Vice President Al Gore calls on us to be 'part of the enormous change our civilization must now undergo ... We must make the rescue of the environment the central organizing principle for civilization'[6], while, according to priest-ecologist Thomas Berry, 'We are not concerned here with some minor adaptations, but with the most serious transformation of human-earth relations that has taken place at least since the classical civilisations were founded'.[7] According to environmentalist Norman Myers: 'We are talking about an entirely new mode of Earthling existence. It will amount to the most seismic shift in outlook since we came out of our cave.'[8]

It is hardly surprising that, imagining themselves to be peering over the brink into extinction, environmental prophets of doom demand drastic measures. Chief amongst these is the halt to economic growth, an end of market economies and industrial development, and an abandoning of the notion of 'progress' understood as improving the quality of life for human beings. Jonathon Porritt, when leader of Friends of the Earth in the UK, was quite blunt about it in his book *The Coming of the Greens* (co-written with David Winner):

> Capitalism itself continues to put Greens in a moral dilemma ... The way most of us in the Western world live now poses a fundamental threat to the planet ... the hydra-headed monster of industrialism has, frankly, slipped its leash. We will not tame it again. It is not so much decapitation that we should be aiming at as the decommissioning of the entire monster.[9]

In June 1992 environmentalists and politicians met in Rio de Janeiro for the United Nations Conference on Environment and Development (UNCED) which became known as the Earth Summit. Its organisers left no doubt that the sort of radical changes they were demanding would have amounted to a New World Order. Maurice Strong, the Secretary General of the Conference, spoke in his opening remarks of:

> ... patterns of production and consumption in the industrialized world that are undermining Earth's life-support systems ... To continue along this pathway could lead to the end of our civilization ... this conference must establish the foundations for effecting the transition to sustainable development. This can only be done through fundamental changes in our economic life and in international economic relations, particularly as between industrialized and developing countries.[10]

In the event the organisers of the Earth Summit were disappointed of their major aims. Critically, President Bush refused to sign the Climate Convention until all references to energy targets had been removed, thus emasculating it. Energy quotas and energy taxes are the Holy Grail of Green politics as they would impose such massive costs as to slow up or reverse economic growth and reduce the standard of living in the West, whilst simultaneously stopping the developing countries from industrialising. These taxes and quotas are demanded as a means of stopping global warming which, as we have said, is not happening anyway. Because President Bush was willing to be the bad guy, attracting the opprobrium of the world's media, we were saved from that at Rio, but we have not always been so lucky in recent years. The banning of CFCs under the Montreal Protocol, originally due to take effect in 2000 but brought forward unilaterally by the USA to 1995, was a panic measure which will impose costs and create problems in innumerable ways, but the Greens demanded action to 'protect' the ozone layer and the politicians gave in. Democratically elected leaders cannot really afford to be depicted as Mr. Polluter.

The document Agenda 21, which was drawn up at Rio, and signed by all of the world leaders attending, contains the extraordinary statement that:

> ... lack of scientific certainty shall not be used as a reason for postponing cost-effective measures to prevent environmental degradation. (Principle 15)

How have we reached this stage at which major policy decisions, which will reduce our standard of living and even our liberties, can be taken without any conclusive scientific evidence that the problems which the measures are supposed to address even exist? If the 'science' of Greenery is really junk science, then what is the mainspring of the movement?

It is the contention of this chapter that the driving force of the Green movement is religious, not scientific. It has grown out of an attempt to promote a view of man and his position in the universe which is not compatible with Christianity. In other words, the Greens have a cosmology of their own which does not square with that of the Bible. Their 'science' is no more than a veneer for this.

Greenery as Religion

The derivation of the word religion is obscure, but it is sometimes said to come from the Latin verb *religare*, meaning to bind together. The adherents to a religion are bound together by certain shared beliefs, and bound into a relationship with God.

Many who concern themselves with environmental issues would say that they have no interest in any spiritual dimension, and simply want to solve certain problems which threaten the ecosystem. However the response to these problems involves the adoption of a lifestyle which is based on strong views regarding the relationship between the human race and the rest of the natural order. This is essentially a religious question, and it has been observed by a number of writers from both the pro- and anti-Green perspective that the life-style options are now so compelling and so numerous as to amount to a system of beliefs, or religion. In his book *Understanding the Present* Bryan Appleyard points out that the committed environmentalist's day 'can be as full of religious observances as a monk's'.[11] Shopping choices are dictated by fears of chemicals and disapproval of factory farming; transport decisions favour bicycles rather than cars; everything possible is recycled. In 'smart' areas the bottle bank has replaced church as the destination for the Sunday morning outing.

Actions can be religiously inspired without explicit references to any creed. As theologian Willis Glover argued in *Biblical Origins of Modern Secular Culture*: 'One's religion is whatever serves as one's ultimate source of meaning'.[12] Gustave Le Bon was equally forthright in *The Crowd: A Study of the Popular Mind*:

> A person is not religious solely when he worships a divinity, but when he puts all the resources of his mind, the complete submission of his will, and the whole-souled ardour of fanaticism at the service of a cause or an individual who becomes the goal and guide of his thoughts and actions.[13]

No one who has listened to tearful encomiums on fallen trees in the rain forest could doubt that, by this definition, Greenery is a religion. In a paper for the Libertarian Alliance on *Environmentalism as Religion* (which he describes as 'Ecolatry') Warren Newman attributes to Greenery those most unattractive attributes of some religious sects, fanaticism and intolerance:

> ... our mood from the 70s and beyond has been to respond to alleged environmental hazards in the way that previous generations had responded to witches ... ICI was now the devil incarnate tempting us to give in to our vanities with hair-sprays and deodorants while the planet was being destroyed ... Anyone who thought CFCs should not be banned was a heretic — a traitor to environmental religious belief. Scientists were expected to conform to the accepted environmental wisdom of the age — the scientific orthodoxy which has become the equivalent of the religious orthodoxy that forced Galileo to agree that the planets go around the earth.[14]

Newman and other observers have identified this tendency towards fanaticism and dogged irrationalism as the only explanation for the fierce adherence by Greens to some policies which are plainly either useless, absurdly expensive or actually counterproductive. Doug Bandow explored this point in a paper for the Competitive Enterprise Institute called *Ecology as Religion: Faith in Place of Fact*:

> The cost of particular policies is seen as irrelevant since the course of action is *morally* required. According to this line of reasoning, it is simply obscene to put a value on elephants, even if doing so, by creating a viable market for ivory, would increase the number of elephants in the long run. Moreover, costly policies may be seen as punishment, a 'desire to purge ourselves of guilt for succeeding too well in taming nature and in generating economic well-being', in Crandall's words. These factors help to explain the widespread enthusiasm for recycling. In fact, much recycling is environmentally wasteful as well as economically inefficient. Polystyrene hamburger clamshells use less energy and generate less air and water pollution to produce. Aseptic packaging requires less energy to manufacture, fill and transport. Recycling newspaper generates toxic sludge. And so on. Yet it is very difficult to objectively examine the desirability of recycling because so many people's commitment to the process is essentially religious.[15]

Robert Nelson gives another example of Green eccentricity which can only be explained by reference to religious conviction in his essay *Environmental Calvinism: The Judeo-Christian Roots of Eco-Theology*:

> Going back to the 1960s, the National Park Service [of the Yellowstone National Park] adopted a policy to destroy mountain goats coming in from the northeast and south sides of the park. Mountain goats coming in from the west side, however, were to be welcomed and protected. One might wonder, what is the difference, since the goats from any side are the same species and would have the same impacts on the park? The answer is that the mountain goats on the west are a natural population, while the goats on the northeast and south sides were introduced some years ago by hunters. Hence, environmental theology decreed that the western goats were permissible in the park, while the northeastern and southern goats would introduce an 'unnatural' presence that demanded their elimination.[16]

13

Although Nelson compares this to the sophistry of medieval scholastics, it is more suggestive of a modern variant on Manichaeism which sees everything man-made as evil and everything natural as good. There is certainly no logic in a position which seeks to discriminate between animals which are biologically of the same species. Even more significant is the policy, pursued in Yellowstone Park since 1972, of only extinguishing man-made fires. Natural fires are allowed to burn in the interests of returning 'the park's ecology, as much as possible, to its natural state'.[17] This 'let-burn' policy was partly responsible for the massive forest fires which destroyed a large part of Yellowstone in 1988. One of the fires, which had been started by a cigarette and therefore did not come under the 'let-burn' rule, could have been extinguished if bulldozers had been allowed into the area to demolish the trees surrounding the blaze. However bulldozers were not permitted to enter the 'wilderness' as their tracks would have left an 'unnatural' look, and the fire eventually consumed half a million acres.[18]

When forest rangers are being called upon to distinguish between a natural and a man-made fire, we have left science behind and exchanged facts for faith. Indeed, some Green activists candidly admit that facts are not the basis of their policy demands. Senator Timothy Wirth of Colorado (now Assistant Secretary of the Interior) claimed that:

> Even if the theory of global warming is wrong, we will be doing the right thing anyway in terms of economic policy and environmental policy.[19]

As the policies proposed to deal with global warming would involve energy taxes and quotas, which would reduce the standard of living, we have to ask in what sense they could be 'right' if the evidence to support them is absent? Presumably they would be 'right' in a moral or religious sense. Gro Harlem Brundtland, Prime Minister of Norway and head of the United Nations commission which produced what became known as *The Brundtland Report* in 1987, claimed that the only way in which people could be made to understand that our present lifestyles are unsustainable and must change would be to persuade them to accept it as 'a religious belief'.[20] It is for this reason that the present environmental debate is conducted in terms which are essentially religious, even when this is not made explicit. It deals with people's values and beliefs, often using the terminology of environmental science as a veneer for these. Indeed Robert Nelson claims in his paper *Unoriginal Sin* that the religious element of environmentalism has come to assume such an important role that:

> ... those who would engage environmentalists in constructive dialogue may find that they have no choice but to enter the realm of theological discussion.[21]

As Nelson points out, because we do not expect public policies to be driven by the religious views of politicians, this theological dynamic of environmentalism is usually kept under wraps. However Vice President Al Gore was quite open about it in his best selling book *Earth in the Balance* in which he states that:

> The more deeply I search for the roots of the global environmental crisis, the more I am convinced that it is an outer manifestation of an inner crisis that is, for lack of a better word, spiritual ... what other word describes the collection of values and assumptions that determine our basic understanding of how we fit into the universe?[22]

Gore is calling us to be saved:

> We each need to assess our own relationship to the natural world and renew, at the deepest level of personal integrity, a connection to it.[23]

The reader can almost hear the cries of 'Amen to that, brother' coming from the back of the hall. 'What does it mean to redefine one's relationship to the sky?'[24] asks the Vice President. Whatever answer may present itself to his mind will be of a religious and not a scientific nature. Gore admits that his concern for the environment is related to 'an intensive search for truths about myself and my life ... More people than ever before are asking "Who are we? What is our purpose?"'[25]

Whilst we can only wish the Vice President success on his quest, it is a matter of some concern that this admission follows his outline for a Global Marshall Plan and a Strategic Environment Initiative (SEI) to save the planet which, if implemented, would have the most dramatic effect on economic growth as well as national sovereignty and individual freedoms. The Plan would involve nothing less than:

> ... large-scale, long-term, carefully targeted financial aid to developing nations, massive efforts to design and then transfer to poor nations the new technologies needed for sustained economic progress, a worldwide program to stabilize world population, and binding commitments by the industrial nations to accelerate their own transition to an environmentally responsible pattern of life.[26]

Although noticeably short on specific recommendations, Gore's Plan would involve the elimination of the internal combustion engine over a 25 year period.[27] Some might wonder if the rest of us should be deprived of that useful invention just because the Vice President is making a spiritual odyssey.

'The Most Anthropocentric Religion'

The fact that the environmental movement is inspired by religious idealism does not, of itself, present problems for Christians. Indeed there is a long and honourable tradition of participation by the people of God in public life, from Daniel and Joseph in the Old Testament to Thomas More, William Wilberforce and Lord Shaftesbury in modern times. The essential question for Christians concerning Green values and practices is: how compatible are they with orthodox Christian teaching? If Greenery has a religious dimension, is this based on Christian insights? Or is it coming from another direction altogether?

In December 1966 American historian Lynn White gave a speech to the American Association for the Advancement of Science entitled *The Historical Roots of our Ecologic Crisis*, which was later published in *Science* magazine.[28] In the light of the current inter-action between the Green movement and the Christian churches it has proved to be prophetic.

White attributed 'the ecologic crisis' to the Christian tradition, which has taught that Man is unique in the order of creation, and that God placed all other creatures under his command:

> Christianity, in absolute contrast to ancient paganism and Asia's reli-

gions (except, perhaps, Zoroastrianism), not only established a dualism of man and nature but also insisted that it is God's will that man exploit nature for his proper ends.[29]

In what was to become a famous phrase White accused Christianity of being 'the most anthropocentric religion the world has seen', because it teaches that man, and only man, is made in God's image and likeness; that there is a complete and fundamental difference between man and the rest of the created order ('Man and nature are two things, and man is master'); and that the rest of the created order is not spiritual:

> In Antiquity every tree, every spring, every stream, every hill had its own *genius loci*, its guardian spirit ... Before one cut a tree, mined a mountain, or dammed a brook, it was important to placate the spirit in charge of that particular situation ... By destroying pagan animism, Christianity made it possible to exploit nature in a mood of indifference to the feelings of natural objects.[30]

White makes an important connection between Christianity and the development of science and technology, which gave practical expression to the Christian view that nature was put there to serve our needs. Because of this connection White regarded science and technology as:

> ... so tinctured with orthodox Christian arrogance towards nature that no solution for our ecologic crisis can be expected from them alone.[31]

The most important thing to say about White's article is that on almost every key point he was absolutely right. Christianity affords man a uniquely exalted station amongst the world's religions. Not only is man made in the image and likeness of God, but God sent his only Son to redeem us from sin and win for us eternal life. This has not been vouchsafed to any animal or plant species.

Furthermore, Christianity has always been implacably opposed to all forms of animism and pantheism which characterised other ancient religions. For the Christian, there is certainly no need to ask permission of rivers to dam them or of mountains to mine them. The mountains and rivers simply have nothing to say on the matter!

17

White was also absolutely correct on another most important point: the Christian origins of science. He did not explore the essential reasons for this nexus, beyond the obvious one to emerge from his line of argument that 'man's effective monopoly on spirit in this world was confirmed [by Christian teaching] and the old inhibitions to the exploitation of nature crumbled'.[32] In other words, people are less likely to be squeamish about putting things under a microscope if they don't think that a god lives in them!

The Christian Matrix of Science

However, White failed to grasp the essential reasons for the Christian matrix of science. Now, thanks to the immense scholarship of the Hungarian Benedictine priest Stanley Jaki, we can appreciate that the link between Christianity and science was the result of certain unique features of Christian doctrine and particularly Christian cosmology.

Jaki has shown that 'science came to an aborted birth in seven great cultures: Chinese, Hindu, Maya, Egyptian, Babylonian, Greek and Arabic'.[33] All made individual discoveries which carried human understanding forward: magnets (the Chinese), decimal notation and the value for zero (India), astronomy and geometry (Ancient Greece). However none were able to develop an ongoing tradition of scientific research and discovery.

Jaki attributes this to two critical features of these ancient cultures which were not present in, and indeed were absolutely shunned and derided by, Christianity. These were the belief in pantheism and the cyclical or repetitive concept of time.

Pantheism is the religious world view which sees god and nature as indistinct. God is not transcendent — outside his creation — but a spirit presence throughout the universe. Science becomes impossible in such a world view because science can only proceed on the understanding that the universe is *rational* and *coherent*. That is to say, things behave in accordance with unchanging laws, which can be discovered through inquiry. To give an example, water always boils at 100 degrees centigrade at sea level. If water were to boil at 99 degrees on one day and 101 degrees on the next there would be no science, because we would not be able to predict anything on the basis of observed experience.

In a culture in which crop failures are blamed on the angry spirits of ancestors, and in which thunder storms and tidal waves represent the amorous squabbles of the gods and goddesses on Mount Olympus, there can be no sustained spirit of scientific enquiry.

The other vital factor which distinguished Christianity from all other ancient cultures was its linear concept of time: God created the universe out of nothing and in time. Indeed the doctrine of *creatio ex nihilo et cum tempore* was from the earliest times regarded as one of the most unique and characteristic aspects of Christian teaching.[34] The Old Testament is based on the salvation history of the Jewish race, which occurred *in time*. Jesus Christ came at a particular point in the history of the Roman Empire, as even the pagan historians attest. Most importantly, time will end at the second coming of Christ.

What all this means, in scientific terms, is that history is progressive: every moment, once it has gone, has gone forever. Things happen once and then never again. This means that there is a significance in a chain of events. They do not happen at random; we can build on past experience. Once an experiment has been carried out it does not have to be repeated over and over again; we can move on to the next stage. It was this linear concept of time which produced the view — essential to science — that progress is possible, and that this can be achieved through learning more about the laws of the universe which are ordained by God.

All ancient cultures other than Judaeo-Christianity were sunk in the hopeless and depressing concept of eternal cycles, the view that things keep repeating themselves, including civilisations and the universe itself. Creatures were seen as being re-incarnated over and over again. In such a world view, nothing has any great significance. It does not matter if opportunities are missed, because they will occur again in another life. The uncertainties and the sense of hopelessness which this world-view engenders are hardly conducive to science. The point is well made by Paul Haffner in his study of Jaki's work, *Creation and Scientific Creativity*:

A major proof of the anti-scientific impact of the organismic world view is found by Jaki in the Babylonian cosmogony, called Enuma Elish … There the actual world order is so uncertain as to call for a yearly expiatory ceremony, the Akitu festival, whose participants tried to ward off cosmic disorder by immersing themselves in ritual orgy … in such a milieu the practical talents of the Babylonians in collecting astronomical data, so useful later for the Greeks, and in developing practical algebra, could not have been expected to rise to a truly scientific level.[35]

In one of his most crucial insights Jaki demonstrates that the theory of inertial motion, which was an essential key to the scientific understanding of a universe in which everything is in motion, was discovered by the Christian scholar John Buridan at the Sorbonne in the fourteenth century *for reasons which were directly related to his theological background*. Buridan's theory was anchored in the Christian understanding of creation out of nothing: every motion must have a beginning, just as the first moment of creation was the beginning of all motion.

What made this all the more significant, in Jaki's view, was the fact that the great Arab scholar Avicenna had come very close to the idea of inertial motion two centuries before, but failed to grasp it. As Paul Haffner explains:

> If the ... formulation [of the law of inertial motion] fell to a Christian medieval scholar, John Buridan, it then becomes almost imperative to suppose that ... there was in the Christian faith in creation a factor that was missing in its Moslem version. The factor was belief in the Incarnation that acted as a powerful safeguard against the lure of pantheism. According to Jaki, 'the crucial insight in Buridan's discussion of impetus is a theological point which is completely alien to Avicenna's thinking'.[36]

The importance of the doctrine of the Incarnation in this respect is that Jesus Christ was the *only begotten* son of God. That is to say, there are no other 'gods' on the earth. The mountains, the forests and the rivers are not divine in any sense. Hence pantheism and animism are rejected.

When Lynn White's article was published in *Science* in 1967 the modern environmental movement was in its infancy. One of the most significant aspects of the article is the fact that, although published in a scientific journal, it is not about science. White gave no evidence to support his claims of an 'ecologic crisis', and it is impossible to tell just what was on his mind. No one was talking about the ozone layer then, and global warming was to be the climate crisis after next. (The big scare of the 1970s was 'the new ice age'.)

Even stranger, perhaps, and of great significance in view of the now considerable anti-scientific bias of Green literature which will be discussed later, was White's rejection of science as a means of solving the problems of the environment: for him science itself was part of the problem. White's real point and purpose in writing the article was to discuss values, more specifically religious values, and more specifically Christianity. His central thesis, stated explicitly, was that the biggest block to the progress of environmental awareness was the Christian attitude towards nature, which he believed still permeated what he called 'post-Christian' Western cultures:

> More science and more technology are not going to get us out of the present ecologic crisis until we find a new religion, or rethink our old one.[37]

As Stephen Fox has shown in his history of environmentalism, White was only making public a strong anti-Christian bias which had existed in the environmental movement since its earliest days in the previous century. Fox shows that John Muir, who later founded the Sierra Club, Ralph Waldo Emerson, and Henry David Thoreau, who were all seminal figures in the development of environmentalism in North America, shared a strong pantheistic faith. Muir wrote to Emerson:

> I invite you to join me in a month's worship with Nature in the high temples of the great Sierra beyond our holy Yosemite … in the name of all the spirit creatures of these rocks and of this whole spiritual atmosphere do not leave us now.[38]

Muir had experienced an unhappy and strict upbringing in which the Bible had been literally beaten into him. Emerson, a Unitarian minister, experienced a crisis of faith and left the church when his 18 year old wife died. Both were looking for alternative religious views, and Emerson developed the mystical doctrine of transcendentalism, based on a romantic attitude towards nature. For Thoreau, nature was not an emanation of God but God itself. 'Is not nature, rightly read, that of which she is commonly taken to be the symbol merely?' he asked.[39]

In his book *Playing God in Yellowstone* Alston Chase describes their new nature religion as:

> ... an eclectic faith of the wilderness. Emerson was its Moses, leading
> the faithful out of the grasp of established religion; Thoreau its Isaiah,
> the prophet; and Muir its David, Guardian of the Promised Land.[40]

However, in the strong Christian culture in which they lived, it was
inadvisable to be too open about any pantheistic sympathies. Stephen
Fox relates that in 1858 Thoreau wrote an article for the *Atlantic* magazine in which he 'declared his faith in the immortality of a pine tree
and its prospects for ascending to heaven. The *Atlantic* ran the piece
without the offending sentence, thereby eliciting a furious letter from
the author'.[41]

The tremendous stir which Lynn White's speech and article caused
can therefore be explained by that fact that he was articulating senti-
ments which had been current amongst environmentalists for decades, but which they had not been able to speak of openly. For many
years pantheism had been the faith which dared not speak its name,
but in the free-and-easy atmosphere of the 1960s environmentalists
felt that they could come out of the closet.

The blame which White attached to Christianity became a constant
theme of Green literature, developing in some cases into a bitter and
sustained assault. Meanwhile, the new religion which White had called
for could be seen emerging in sections of the environmental movement. It was, as he had predicted, a religious world view based on
pantheism and animism which would redefine the relationship between man and the natural order, supposedly to save the planet from
our depredations.

The Decline of Faith

It is perhaps superfluous to observe that there has been a dramatic
drop in the support for mainstream Christianity in the West during the
latter part of this century. In the decades since the Second World War
churches have emptied and hundreds have been declared redundant.
Ingenious architects have turned church buildings into offices, shops
and houses. Church attendance has declined to the point at which
only a small minority of the population in Britain regularly visit a
place of worship. The reasons for this decline are beyond the scope of

this book, but the consequences are not.

Because man is a spiritual being he can never be satisfied by purely materialistic creeds, whether Marxist or capitalist. No secular or materialistic creed can answer those questions which have presented themselves to his mind since the beginning of time. Where do we come from? What purpose is there in life? What happens after death? The study of anthropology is sufficient to tell us that the religious instinct is so deeply ingrained in human nature that atheistic societies are not only rare but almost impossible to find before the twentieth century.

As support for Christianity has declined, people have looked elsewhere to meet this basic human need to worship, or at least to have something to believe in. For some, the passionate support of a political creed may act as a substitute for religion. There is no doubt that Marxism filled this gap in the lives of many Western intellectuals, who felt obliged to defend it long after it had become obvious that it did not work. For others, art has become a religion. But as Richard D. North, then environment correspondent for *The Independent*, explained, environmentalism provided a new god for many of its adherents:

> An awful lot of us just need to worship something. But in order to be able to worship, you have to be able to find something outside of yourself — and better than yourself. God is a construct for that. So is nature. We are falling in love with the environment as an extension to and in lieu of having fallen out of love with God. As it happens, it makes for a pretty deficient religion, but as an object of worship, nature takes some beating.[42]

Bill McKibben makes this explicit in his book *The End of Nature* in which he writes of the 'crisis of belief' which has characterised modern times and then claims that 'many people, including me, have overcome it to a greater or lesser degree by locating God in nature'.[43] Robert Nelson has described how:

> ... nature becomes for McKibben a substitute for the Christian God; if Friedrich Nietzsche a century earlier warned of dire consequences of the death of God, the end of nature today for McKibben and for many others of environmental faith would have much the same meaning.[44]

The Age of Aquarius

In one of his most-quoted remarks G.K. Chesterton pointed out that, when people lose faith in God, they don't believe in nothing, they believe in anything. His aphorism has certainly proved to be true for our times. As the Christian churches have emptied out, many people have sought to meet their spiritual needs by subscribing to religious faiths outside of the world's mainstream religions altogether. This accounts for the dramatic rise in support in recent years for every variety of spiritualism and the occult, including witchcraft and satanism.

The seemingly unconnected phenomena of occultism, witchcraft, tarot cards, astrology, crystals, transcendental meditation, yoga and other imports from Eastern religions are all manifestations of a phenomenon which can now clearly be seen as a challenge to Christianity: the New Age Movement.

It is difficult either to describe or to criticise the New Age because it has no formal structure: no leader, no headquarters, and no statement of doctrine. However there are sufficient common threads running through New Age literature for us to discern key themes.

It is syncretist, which is to say that it picks bits and pieces from other world religions. Its main influences, however, are Eastern, derived from Hinduism and Buddhism. It teaches that God is not an individual being, outside of his creation, but a force of infinite intelligence and consciousness throughout creation. This is pantheism.

It teaches that Jesus was not *the* Christ, but *a* Christ. He was a holy man, but no more than many others. Furthermore Christ is in all of us: we are all Christs and we are all god. Sin, guilt and repentance are all behind us. We are entering the Age of Aquarius, when we will be able to achieve anything by discovering the spiritual force within us.

In almost every important respect the New Age is diametrically opposed to Christianity. Unfortunately this has not prevented many Christians from being drawn in to what they see as a religious development for our times. The New Age infiltration of the church has been documented in books like Randy England's *The Unicorn in the Sanctuary*[45] and Constance Cumbey's *The Hidden Dangers of the Rainbow.*[46]

Randy England shows how New Age practices such as self-hypnosis, transcendental meditation, 'visualisation' and yoga are promoted by Christian bookshops and in Christian parishes, even though they conflict with basic Christian principles. Some Christians even defend the widespread New Age belief in re-incarnation.

Constance Cumbey's exposé of the New Age challenge to Christianity shows how New Agers pray to 'spirit guides' from Lucifer to Pan, and quotes from 'Christian' New Age books which contain the sort of rank heresies which would be the stock-in-trade of occult literature. Mrs. Cumbey traces the intellectual origins of the New Age back to Madame Blavatsky and the Theosophists of the late nineteenth century, and shows how their ideas gained currency through occult publishing houses, and through the 'networking' of like-minded individuals. However, Mrs. Cumbey's book misses out on an important point. Madame Blavatsky was a crank and the Theosophists were regarded as eccentrics on the fringes of society. Their mystical writings and weird prophesies held no interest for policy makers; in fact their influence on public policy was nil. Even the spread of heretical ideas in the churches through key New Age figures like Thomas Merton and the French Jesuit Pierre Teilhard de Chardin can hardly be regarded as a political success. In the West politicians pay little attention to the writings of theologians, orthodox or otherwise.

However, in spite of its lack of a formal organisational structure, the New Age movement promotes certain political goals which have now entered the arena of public debate. These include one world government, a single currency, universal taxation, the redistribution of wealth through a New World Economic Order and the allocation of food and other resources through global agencies. Such aims are not regarded as unreasonable by many who now figure on the world stage. So what has changed since the days of Madame Blavatsky?

In order to achieve political influence it was necessary to talk about other things than 'inner lights' and 'spirit friends'. There had to be real practical issues to which these spiritual 'insights' could be attached, the sort of issues which politicians could reasonably be expected to address. The supposed collapse of the ecosystem under the impact of human exploitation has provided these issues, like warding off climate change. The Green movement articulated, in terms which seemed convincing to politicians, the need for practical measures which would, at the same time, carry forward the New Age agenda.

For example, at the United Nations Earth Summit in Rio de Janeiro, the case for a world authority to overrule national sovereignty was put by Michel Rocard, a former Prime Minister of France:

> We need a real world authority, to which should be delegated the fol-
> low-up of the international decisions, like the treaties signed [at Rio]
> ... This authority must have the capacity to have its decisions obeyed
> ... Obviously, this supra-national authority must be a world author-
> ity.[47]

There is a widespread notion that pollution and environmental degradation know no boundaries, and that this must spell the end of the
nation state, as a supra-national authority will be required to deal with
the problems. It is the modern guise for the pursuit of one world government which goes back to the earliest days of New Age mysticism.

Politicians who canvass these ideas may or may not have heard of
the Age of Aquarius. They would certainly not want to make policy
proposals to the public justified by appeals to the 'inner light', spirit
energies and the seven nerve centres. The policies can only be presented on the basis of the 'real' issues which environmentalism is
supposed to supply.

It is only against the background of the New Age mysticism which
informs the environmental movement that we can understand the
motivation for the political campaigns. Many of the goals which are
being pursued in the name of the environment will not only curtail
economic growth, but would also represent ever-tightening restric-
tions on the liberty of the individual. Some of the most important are,
at best, unnecessary and at worst a real threat to human well-being,
such as energy taxes and laws which favour destructive animals and
even vermin over human beings under the guise of preserving 'endangered species'.[48] To get people in the frame of mind to take such
unpleasant medicine a formidable threat is required: everything hinges
on the prospect of an imminent ecological collapse. Without it, the
whole agenda descends into the pathetic silliness of Madame Blavatsky
and the Theosophists.

In at the Deep End

To present the whole of the Green movement as simply a new guise
for Madame Blavatsky, or the political wing of the New Age Movement, would be a gross oversimplification. There are numerous other

strands, some of them hostile to the New Age. For example, at the extreme edge of the Green movement we find Deep Ecology which is based on what they call biological egalitarianism. This is the view that all parts of nature have equal rights, not only animals, but rocks, rivers, and the sky. Deep Ecologists have a contempt for mainstream environmental groups which seek to make the world a better place *for humans*, and even oppose the New Age movement as being too human-centred. As Christopher Manes explains in his book *Green Rage: Radical Environmentalism and the Unmaking of Civilization*, for Deep Ecologists the very idea of civilisation is repulsive with its 'unwarranted anthropocentrism, its privileging of technological progress, its claims of hegemony over the natural world'.[49] Manes quotes John Davis, the editor of *Earth First!*, who advocates a return to the hunter-gatherer lifestyles of fifteen thousand years ago,[50] and Mike Roselle who describes Deep Ecology as a new civil rights movement 'for all people. The tree people, rock people, deer people, grass-hopper people and beyond'.[51] Manes also cites the view of sociologist Lynton Caldwell that the modern environmental movement represents a sort of second Copernican revolution. In the first we were forced to abandon the idea that the earth is at the centre of the universe (geocentrism); in the second, we are being asked to give up the view that man is superior to the rest of creation (anthropocentrism).[52]

This is just as much a religious position as the New Age movement, as it still turns on the consideration of the origins, role and destiny of the human person — a spiritual question of the most profound significance. In spite of the well-known run in between Galileo and the church, the revelation that the earth goes around the sun had no theological implications, when properly understood. Christian cosmology was in no way compromised. The abandoning of 'anthropocentrism' would have far more serious implications.

Although Deep Ecology represents an extreme of the Green movement, it remains the case that the view of man as nothing very special, and in some ways something rather disgraceful, is one of the most important components of the environmental creed. As we have seen, some of the nineteenth century founding fathers of environmentalism were already a long way down the road to anti-human pantheism, but they kept these views largely to themselves. They could not have expected to attract popular support at the time by speaking what many would have regarded as blasphemy.

In 1992 *The Illustrated London News* published a special edition to celebrate its 150th anniversary in which writers were asked to look back over the period to see how attitudes had changed towards their subjects. TV naturalist David Attenborough was asked to cover wild-life, and he came to the conclusion that the major difference between the attitudes of the early Victorians towards animals and our own was that they had no doubts that God had created the animals for the benefit of human beings. Now we are not so sure. Attenborough called his article 'What Are We Doing Here?', which is a theological rather than a scientific question, and not one which would have troubled the founding members of the Royal Society for the Prevention of Cruelty to Animals (RSPCA) in 1824. They knew.

This feeling that environmental problems are all rooted in the phenomenon of man getting above himself is the common thread which now runs through every aspect of the Green debate, from architectural conservation and nuclear power to transport policy and zoos. The present environmental crisis is seen to be the result of the Christian arrogance towards nature, which is derived from man's uniquely exalted status in the natural order. This in turn has led to the rise of science, which has allowed man to exploit nature to satisfy his greed.

A New Renaissance

As Doug Bandow has shown in a paper for the Competitive Enterprise Institute, the constant denigration of Christianity and the call to replace it with something more earth-centred have become standard themes of Green writers. In his book *The Rebirth of Nature* Rupert Sheldrake attacks the Judaeo-Christian tradition for having 'always emphasized the supremacy of the male God' in contrast to mother earth. He calls for 'a new renaissance' in which we 'acknowledge the animistic traditions of our ancestors'.[53] Jeremy Rifkin and Ted Howard argue in their book *Entropy: Into the Greenhouse World* that 'the traditional Christian approach to nature has been a major contributing factor to ecological destruction' and they call for 'a radical reformulation of Christian theology' to incorporate aspects of Eastern religions.[54] James Nash of the Churches Center for Theology and Public Policy calls upon the Christian churches to 'eradicate the last vestiges of these ecologically ruinous myths'.[55]

This view of Christianity as essentially destructive has become so widespread that Thomas Clarke, an American Jesuit priest, can even say:

> I do accept the scandal that the earth has suffered more from Christians than from any other religious group ... Has Christianity been a blessing or a curse to this earth? That is a very, very hard question for me, but I am grateful that at least I have come to the point where I can really listen to it in God's presence as a question.[56]

The spirituality of the New Age Movement, in contrast, appears to offer the opportunity which Green writers are calling for, to 'redefine' our relationship with the planet. Because of the New Age belief in pantheism and animism, as well as the important question of reincarnation, it is seen as much more 'planet friendly'. It offers a means of, on the one hand, cutting man down to size by merging him with the rest of nature, while at the same time making people feel good about themselves by telling them that they are all Christs and all gods.

New Age meets the requirements of Greenery so well that it is now extremely difficult to discuss the Green movement without referring to New Age, and vice-versa. Green spirituality is essentially New Age spirituality. This makes serious problems for Christians who want to be involved with the Green movement without letting go of their beliefs. Even Chris Seaton in his book *Whose Earth?*, in which he goes to great lengths to be fair to New Age and dismisses much of the criticism of it as 'conspiracy-hunting', is forced to admit to concern about the way in which the Christian Ecology Link dabbles in such concepts as 'the cosmic Christ', global spirituality, and exploring 'the God within':

> Sadly, these concerns were only reinforced by the choice of one of the main speakers to the 1991 CEL conference, a Roman Catholic priest whose teaching was regarded by many as mainstream New Age![57]

Creation Spirituality

The aim of Green spirituality is to re-assess the relationship between man and nature, or as Jeremy Rifkin puts it, to 'resacralize our relationship' to the planet.[58] One of the main approaches to this end has been the development of what is called creation-centred spirituality, of which the most famous exponent has been Matthew Fox, a Dominican priest and Director of the Institute in Culture and Creation Spirituality in California. Fox is a controversial character who has a witch called Starhawk on the staff of his Centre, and who claims that his spiritual director is his dog.[59] He was dismissed from the Dominican Order in March 1993.

The starting point of his best-selling book *Original Blessing* is that the human race requires 'a new religious paradigm',[60] and that creation-centred spirituality fits the bill. He claims that we have to get away from what he calls the fall/redemption model of religion which emphasises human sinfulness and our need of redemption through Jesus Christ. He believes that this concentration on original sin, for which he blames St. Augustine, has distracted us from the 'original blessing' of nature:

> In religion we have been operating under the model that humanity, and especially sinful humanity, was the center of the spiritual universe. This is not so ... the time has come to let anthropocentrism go, and with it to let the preoccupation with human sinfulness give way to attention to divine grace.[61]

This is not to say that Fox doesn't believe in sin. He certainly does, although not in the sense in which most Christians would understand the word. For Fox, sin is the result of a lack of respect for nature:

> Sin ... would consist in injuring creation and doing harm to its balance and harmoniousness ... It represents the most basic injustice, that of humanity to its own source, the earth ... religion's sin of omission and of silent complicity during the centuries in which human/divine creativity was used to ... wipe out millions of species — this must be confessed openly.[62]

Fox clearly sees himself as a prophet, and this view is shared by his numerous followers. Like others in this line of business, he is perhaps unfortunate in attracting disciples who go much further than he does himself.

One of his principal followers is Thomas Berry, a Passionist priest who describes himself as a 'geologian' and is involved with the running of the Holy Cross Centre for Ecology and Spirituality in Ontario. His book *Befriending the Earth: a Theology of Reconciliation Between Humans and the Earth*, must rank as one of the strangest outpourings of an ordained Christian minister.

To say that Berry sees the present moment as a turning point would be an understatement. He believes that the scope of the present eco-logical catastrophe is so great that we 'have the whole planet at stake ... something that no one faced in former centuries'.[63]

He also claims that we are at the end of the 'Cenozoic' period which has lasted for 65 million years and at the beginning of the 'Ecozoic' period, and that in this period all of the 'human modalities' which have functioned in the past, like Christianity and Biblical revelation, will have to be re-assessed.[64]

One of the 'conditions' of this Ecozoic Age is:

> ... a sense of the earth as having a voice, as speaking to us. We must
> have the sense, in our communication with nature, that it is not simply
> trees or water speaking to us, but it is the earth itself speaking to us.[65]

Berry believes that traditional religions are inadequate to cope with the scale of the ecological crisis, and that Christianity has been fairly useless in that respect anyway. He regards the Ten Commandments as inadequate, as none of them are about the environment, and criticises the Apostles' Creed on the same basis. Christian baptism is unsatis-factory because it does not spell out our relationship with the natural world: he prefers the rite of initiation of the Omaha Indians who present an infant to the four regions of the universe.[66]

Berry also suggests that we should give up the Bible for twenty years and abandon what he calls our 'obsessive concern' with Jesus Christ: 'We need to let go. *If Jesus is who he is supposed to be*, he will show up'[67] (emphasis added).

It would be superfluous to comment on the unorthodox nature of these views. Suffice it to say that Berry is not a fringe figure: his work is quoted with approval by many writers on Green spirituality in the UK, including some Christians.

Multi-Faith Worship

As we have seen, the New Age movement which informs so much of

Green spirituality is syncretist: it mixes up the environmentally-friendly parts from different world religions, as well as encouraging an openness towards the paganism and animism of primitive peoples. For example, Thomas Berry believes that 'the salvation of Christians lies in the unassimilated elements of paganism'.[68]

The religious ceremonies and festivals which are now quite frequently celebrated by Green organisations seem to represent ecumenism to the power of a million: Christianity, Hinduism, Sikhism and Islam are all mixed up, as if there were no important differences between them. Anyone who raised the possibility at such a gathering that Christianity might be true and the other world religions only imperfect approximations to the truth would, no doubt, find himself as welcome as the man who asked for a pork chop at a Bar Mitzvah in the Bateman cartoon.

The World Wide Fund for Nature (WWF), formerly the World Wildlife Fund, has led the way in this area by establishing a Network on Conservation and Religion. It was launched as the result of a gathering in Assisi in 1986 of representatives of different faiths, each of whom contributed to a Declaration on Religion and Nature.[69] According to Prince Philip, the International President of WWF whose idea the gathering had been, the event signified that 'a new and powerful alliance has been forged between the forces of religion and the forces of conservation'.[70] At a celebration in the Basilica on 29 September a Muslim muezzin was called upon to praise Allah, and this was followed by a Hindu dance, a prayer chanted by three Tibetan monks, readings from Hindu scriptures and the Koran, and a prayer to Shiva, the Hindu god of destruction and reproduction.[71]

In September 1989 the WWF took over the whole of Canterbury Cathedral, its precincts and other church property in Canterbury for a Celebration of Faith and the Environment. The promotional literature announced that 'the world's great faiths ... are working together ... through shared pilgrimage; conference; performance; music; *worship*; exhibitions ... to celebrate the best in our relationship with nature'[72] (emphasis added). Buddhists, Sikhs and members of other faiths were practicing their own rites and rituals, while a liturgy conducted in the Cathedral to welcome the environmental 'pilgrims' contained no reference to Jesus Christ. The booklet produced for the Sunday morning Communion service, taken by the Archbishop of Canterbury, suggested 'resources for reflection' from Baha'i, Buddhist, Confucian,

Hindu, Moslem and Sikh writings.

One of the highlights of the weekend was a Celebration of the Forest which took place in the Cathedral on the Saturday night. The choir from St Augustine's Roman Catholic High School in Billington performed an oratorio called *Yanamamo*, based on the beliefs of rain forest Indians. The holy men and women buried under the pavement must have been surprised to hear the children sing 'The trees have power. We worship them ... We live because they give us life'.[73]

A group of evangelical Christians led by Rev. Tony Higton of Action for Biblical Witness to our Nation (ABWON) protested outside the Cathedral against this use of church property for acts of worship by members of other faiths. When they gathered outside the main entrance to sing hymns praising Jesus as Lord they were escorted off the premises by security guards, and were informed that the police had been called. Rev. Higton wrote to the *Church Times*:

> I sometimes ponder on a future scenario of an apostate church persecuting orthodox believers over this interfaith compromise issue. In connection with this prospect the Canterbury weekend was most illuminating.[74]

The Dean and the Archbishop of Canterbury refused to accept that anything improper has taken place. However, the God of Abraham, Isaac and Jacob is a jealous God: 'You shall have no gods except me' (Exod.20:3). The punishment of those who bowed down before false gods was inevitable. Nor was this exclusivity of worship in any way modified by Christ in the New Covenant:

> I am the Way, the Truth, and the Life. No one can come to the Father except through me.
>
> John 14:6

Nothing could be more plain in the history of both the Jewish and the Christian faiths than this essential separateness from other spiritualities. It was one of the most distinguishing characteristics of the Jews which both puzzled and infuriated their Roman rulers. It was the motivating force behind the Christian tradition of evangelism. It was the inspiration of the martyrs. Quite simply, we are not entitled to make a pick'n'mix of the world's religions just because we are worried about the rain forests.

The multi-faith mish-mash of the Canterbury event was far from unique. Such services and events have been held in many other churches, and not only under the auspices of the WWF. For Christians all such events are highly risky, because it is sometimes by no means clear just who is being worshipped. The attitude towards nature — or Nature — is also sometimes worryingly ambivalent in these services. In 1987 the WWF organised a strange Harvest Festival, retitled Creation and Harvest, in Winchester Cathedral. The purpose of the event was to remind people that:

> ... our increase in harvest is the result of the elimination of wildlife ... the rooting up of age-old hedgerows and the loss of thousands of years of topsoil.[75]

The procession bearing the fruits of the earth was met in the aisle by the Dean with these words:

> No. Come no further. Your offering is not acceptable in the sight of God

The gifts were then placed on a table while two actors extemporised over their environmental costs.

> They explained the evils of wheat and dairy overproduction, deforestation for financial gain, single-crop economies, over-fishing and erosion ... After repentance came the act of communion. In usual communion services, sins are confessed and God asked for forgiveness, with the priest giving absolution. In this case, however, Dean Beeson, although able to give absolution for sins committed against God, said the seeking of forgiveness had to go further: 'As a priest, I can offer absolution from God for those sins for which we ask his forgiveness', he said. 'We shall not know if Nature has forgiven us for many years to come'.[76]

If reported accurately, this was a most extraordinary statement. Christians believe that sin represents a dislocation in the relationship between God and man, a failure to respond to the free offer of God's love. However, God's forgiveness is always available to the repentant

34

sinner, unconditionally. We cannot sin against 'Nature' and 'Nature' cannot forgive us.

A Creation Festival Liturgy held in Coventry Cathedral the following year, also organised by the WWF, went even further, including the prayer:

> Our brothers and sisters of the creation, the mighty trees, the broad oceans, the air, the earth, the creatures of creation, forgive us and reconcile us to you.[77]

Whilst no one would want to accuse the Cathedral authorities involved of participating in nature worship, Christians need to be alert to the risks involved in personifying Nature in acts of worship, even if the intention is only symbolic. Even the suggestion of unintentional nature worship is something which should fill Christians with foreboding. St. Paul warned us in the strongest terms against regarding nature as divine. He told the inhabitants of pagan Rome that God has revealed himself to us through the wonders of creation, but his wrath will be unleashed against those who have turned away from the creator to worship the creation:

> The more they called themselves philosophers, the more stupid they grew, until they exchanged the glory of the immortal God for a worthless imitation, for the image of mortal man, of birds, of quadrupeds and reptiles. That is why God left them to their filthy enjoyments and the practices with which they dishonour their own bodies, since they have given up divine truth for a lie and have worshipped and served creatures instead of the creator.
>
> Rom.1:22-23

The Christian and the Environment

In 1992 the WWF sponsored the publication of five books on Hinduism/Buddhism/Judaism/Christianity/Islam and Ecology. Reviewing them for *The Guardian*, religious affairs correspondent Walter Schwartz noted that Hinduism and Buddhism came off best, as they make no distinct separation between the human person and the rest of nature. In contrast, what Schwartz calls 'the three later religions' did not fit so easily into the Green mould.[78]

Whatever the merits or demerits of the Christian contribution to this particular series,[79] there has been a serious attempt by Christian writers and theologians in recent years to address the issue of a Christian theology of the environment.

We have already looked at a number of Green approaches to spirituality which are, by Christian standards, highly unorthodox. However, we have to acknowledge that the domination of the field by the proponents of various weird and esoteric fringe religions is partly due to the fact that the Christian churches have had so little to say about creation and cosmology in recent times. This is a deficiency which a number of current publications are now addressing.

Christian writers who are not sympathetic to New Age or to pantheism and animism have attempted to present a Christian response to environmental issues. They have insisted that Christianity is *not* anthropocentric — the key charge of Lynn White's 1967 article which has been repeated endlessly ever since. Christianity is *theocentric*: its teachings are based on the concept of an omniscient and omnipotent God and creator, who has revealed himself to us and who has given us the 'ground rules' for the sort of life which will be pleasing to him, and which will gain for us eternal life. Christians do *not* regard man as the measure of all things: that is a humanist doctrine.

Furthermore a lot of work has been done on the so-called Dominion Covenant of Genesis, made between God and Adam and Eve:

> Be fruitful, multiply, fill the earth and conquer it. Be masters of the fish of the sea, the birds of heaven and all living animals on the earth.
>
> Gen.1:28

The covenant was repeated with Noah in even stronger terms:

> Be fruitful, multiply and fill the earth. Be the terror and dread of all the wild beasts and all the birds of heaven, of everything that crawls on the ground and all the fish of the sea; they are handed over to you. Every living and crawling thing shall provide food for you, no less than the foliage of plants.
>
> Gen.9:1-2

Some Christian writers have argued that these covenants are based on a concept of stewardship rather than arbitrary and total power. In his book *God is Green* Ian Bradley shows that this idea of stewardship is not new by quoting the seventeenth century author Sir Matthew Hale:

> The end of man's creation was that he should be the viceroy of the great God of heaven and earth in this inferior world; his steward, bailiff or farmer of this goodly farm of the lower world. Only for this reason was man invested with power, authority, right, dominion, trust and care, to correct and abridge the excesses and cruelties of the fiercer animals, to give protection and defence to the mansuete [tame] and useful, to preserve the species of divers vegetables, to improve them and others, to correct the redundance of unprofitable vegetables, to preserve the face of the earth in beauty, usefulness and fruitfulness.[80]

Who could resist an appeal to correct the redundance of unprofitable vegetables? Unfortunately, in his eagerness for 'making Christianity environment-friendly once again',[81] Bradley, like other Green Christian writers, is sometimes tempted to load more modern interpretations onto scripture than the text will bear. For example, he believes that:

> The biblical account of the fall could indeed be read as a story of what happens when Adam ceases organic husbandry and introduces intensive methods of agriculture.[82]

Really? We used to think it was about sin. And what are we to make of this plaintive rhetorical question:

> When Jesus told his disciples, 'In as much as ye did it to one of the least of your brethren ye did it to me', was he perhaps indicating that we should feed the dumb animals as well as the starving in the Third World and pray for endangered species of plant and insect as well as for homeless and suffering humanity?[83]

The short answer to that is no. However Bradley is so impressed by his own line of argument that he goes on to claim:

> Perhaps just as important as our responsibility to articulate the prayers of the dumb animals and inanimate elements is our role as fellow suf-

ferers with the threatened rain forests and the species doomed to extinction.[84]

Although this is clearly an extremist position, Bradley has raised an important point with his view that humans should regard themselves as fellow-sufferers with trees, because the attitude towards trees is in many ways the very touchstone of Greenery.

Talking to the Trees

Love of trees is the essential attribute for every self- respecting Green, from the most publicity-conscious politician to the most idealistic viewer of *Captain Planet*. Our hearts are supposed to bleed every time an axe is taken to a tree, especially if it is in Amazonia. But why? Is it because people are afraid we will run short of wood? If so, this is a groundless fear. According to the United Nations Food and Agriculture Organisation, the total forested area of the globe increased from 3.52 billion hectares in 1949 to 4.05 billion hectares in 1989. It is true that in some countries very unwise logging programmes have despoiled the landscape and caused other problems, but these can be rectified by replanting. The claim that whole types of forest are facing annihilation is absurd and not based on scientific data. Tropical forests still cover over 1.7 billion hectares of the earth's surface,[85] more than 13 percent of the global land area.

So why does the very mention of deforestation arouse the sort of sensations usually associated with rape and child abuse? Is it because trees are seen as having some value in themselves, quite separate from their usefulness to human beings? Are trees spiritual? Jonathon Porritt, for many years Director of Friends of the Earth in the UK, describes himself as an 'unreconstructed dendrophile' and claims that 'trees are my spiritual connection to the earth',[86] while a leaflet produced by Friends of the Earth complained of the 'murder' of tropical rain forests. But how can a forest be murdered, unless it is a sentient, intelligent being? And what does the latter assumption tell us about the religious viewpoint of those who hold it? Writing in the *Earth First!* magazine George Wuerthner even denied that the US Forest Service could own old-growth trees any more than a southern plantation owner could own slaves.[87]

In his 1967 article for *Science* magazine Lynn White proved to be prophetic in this, as in so many other respects, concerning the development of the Green movement. He identified trees as a special concern for environmentalists, and a stumbling block for Christians:

> To a Christian a tree can be no more than a physical fact. The whole concept of the sacred grove is alien to Christianity ... For nearly 2 millennia Christian missionaries have been chopping down sacred groves, which are idolatrous because they assume spirit in nature.[88]

This criticism of Christian missionaries for cutting down the sacred groves of paganism has been endlessly repeated by Green writers (including Christians) since White's day. It is something about which Christian Greens are deeply embarrassed, and St. Boniface (675?-755), the English missionary to Germany, is regarded as the chief culprit. According to Thomas Berry:

> The historical reality is that Christians, like St Boniface ... cut down the oak trees deemed sacred by the pagans ... Today that would be absurd. The unassimilated elements of paganism have so much to offer us in establishing an intimate rapport with the natural world.[89]

And yet the much-maligned St. Boniface had scriptural authority for his actions. The author of Deuteronomy gave very definite instructions to God's people who found themselves in lands where other gods were worshipped:

> ... deal with them like this: tear down their altars, smash their standing-stones, cut down their sacred poles and set fire to their idols.
>
> Deut.7:5

St. Paul rams home the point:

> Light and darkness have nothing in common. Christ is not the ally of Beliar ... The temple of God has no common ground with idols.
>
> 2 Cor.6:14-16

It would be more difficult to find scriptural justification for Fr. Berry's notions of absorbing the 'unassimilated elements of paganism'! However, as we have seen, Berry is a fairly off-the-wall character who goes much further than other Christian Greens. Unfortunately, even amongst the Christian writers who do not admire paganism and animism, we find traces of an attitude towards trees which seems to regard them as more than just a source of wood. For example, Fr. Sean McDonagh argues in *The Greening of the Church* that:

> The Church should mobilize people at every level to protect and conserve the forests. Catechetical literature and liturgical celebrations, like tree-planting liturgies or harvest festivals, can touch people's hearts ... Lands surrounding churches and schools should, where possible, be planted with trees, rather than be cultivated as lawns.[90]

We are entitled to ask, why should the minister have his windows darkened by trees if he would rather have a view across lawns and flower beds? Trees are not necessary for Christian worship.

The 'Paradigm' of Science

The Green movement has provoked demands for a radical reorganisation of human societies in order to bring them into closer harmony with the earth. This would inevitably involve the most profound economic and political consequences if the policies of world government and a halt to economic growth were taken seriously.

However, the Greens are now making another demand which is, in a way, even more extraordinary given that they claim to be a movement based on scientific insights: some of the more radical elements are actually demanding an end to science.

Edward Goldsmith, the founder of *The Ecologist*, has written a rather lumbering attempt at a spiritual text called *The Way: an ecological world view* in which he hands down *ex cathedra* certain commandments or principles for living in The Way of ecology. A brief glance at the contents list is sufficient to grasp the flow of the argument: 'Ecology is a faith', 'Gaia is alive', 'There is no fundamental barrier separating man and other living things'. This is all fairly standard Green stuff, but the most interesting aspect of the book is its insistence that our ecological crisis is due to what Goldsmith calls 'the world-view of modernism and the closely associated paradigm of science'.[91] Modernism is bad, in Goldsmith's eyes, because it rests on the assumption that progress is achievable and desirable. This progress (for man) is not really progress at all because it conflicts with the needs of the planet, and science is bad because it represents the means of achieving the desired progress:

> ... economic progress cannot occur without disrupting the critical order of the natural world. As the world-view of modernism and the associated paradigm of science slowly developed to rationalize and hence legitimize this anti-evolutionary enterprise, the notion of balance and harmony was increasingly marginalized ... In the light of the analysis provided in this book, however, human evolution, or progress, is the very negation of evolution, or the Gaian process, and is best referred to as anti-evolution.[92]

So far so standard. Any Green writer hoping to be taken seriously by his target audience would have to be against economic development. However, the interesting thing here is Goldsmith's use of the term 'the paradigm of science'. A paradigm is a pattern or model: it explains things. The cosmologies of all of the world's religions are paradigms, because they attempt to explain how the universe came to be what it is. But a paradigm is not a matter of empirical proof: you can choose whether or not you want to believe it. Buddhists would not accept the Christian paradigm, and vice versa. Goldsmith is suggesting that science is *just one way* of looking at the universe, with no more exclusive a claim to truthfulness than any one religion. Indeed, Goldsmith regards science *as a religion*:

> Science, in many respects, is just another religion ... it has ... substituted faith in modern science for faith in conventional religion.[93]

Like any other religion, then, you can choose not to believe in it. If you dislike what science is doing to the world, you can avoid it by taking another world view:

> ... so long as we argue within the accepted 'conceptual framework' of the reigning paradigm ... we can never persuade people either to accept a new idea or to abandon an old one ... For people to accept the principles listed in this book, it is the paradigm of science itself that must be abandoned, and hence the world view of modernism which it faithfully reflects; and they must be replaced by the world-view of

41

ecology ... It must, in fact, involve a change akin to a religious conversion.[94]

This is really an extraordinary view. Science deals with objective reality. It seeks to discover the ways in which the universe works by putting forward explicit propositions which can be tested and either accepted or rejected on the basis of observed experience. To suggest that science is a matter of faith or personal conviction is to suggest that individuals can choose to either accept or reject reality. Those who reject reality have traditionally been regarded as mad.

Science and Sorcery

Just a few months before Goldsmith handed down his scriptures a book by journalist Bryan Appleyard had been published which covered some of the same ground. *Understanding the Present* accuses science of smashing religion without putting anything in its place to give meaning to our lives. Appleyard is quite explicit that science is a product of Western culture which has achieved world domination at the expense, as he sees it, of other ways of looking at things:

> ... there is no Japanese science as distinct from American science. There is only one science and, in time, all cultures bow to its omniscience and to its refusal to co-exist ... No Buddhist, Muslim or Confucian culture has produced a better way of increasing crop yields, curing disease or killing people than the Western way. So those cultures, when they wish to eat, live or fight, turn to the West's science.[95]

Appleyard believes that science has 'left us with the aching, anguished loneliness of scientific man in a universe which, in some ghastly parody of the original fall from grace, his knowledge had stripped of goodness or meaning'.[96] As an example of the way in which science destroys religious faith he posits the case of a Western doctor who comes upon the sick child of parents in an isolated non-Western culture. By administering penicillin he can save the child's life, but at the same time he risks destroying the people's culture because:

> When local wisdom is humiliated by science and local culture is drawn into scientific civilization, it is difficult to believe that what remains

can continue to be a unique culture in any meaningful sense ... the truth is that all the artifacts, clothes and rituals were diminished at the moment the penicillin was first administered.[97]

For Appleyard it is a moral dilemma; should the child be allowed to die in the hope that the culture can be saved? However, from a Christian point of view, the dilemma is an imaginary one, because science only destroys religious belief which is based on ignorance and superstition. Of course, in the example given, the witch doctor would lose face and no one would go to him any more because they would all want antibiotics, but this is simply an exposé of the deceitfulness of paganism.

Christianity has nothing to fear from science because it is a faith based on reason. Christians are not called upon to accept a view of the world which is irrational and superstitious. On the contrary, the Book of Wisdom insists that God gave us the power to come to know him by applying our ordinary faculties of reason and observation to the world around us (Ws.13:1-9). St Paul emphasised the point in his letter to the Romans:

> Ever since God created the world his everlasting power and deity — however invisible — have been there for the mind to see in the things he has made.
>
> Rom.1: 20.

As Stanley Jaki and others have shown, the conjunction of science and Western culture was not a geographical accident, because the viable and self-sustaining scientific enterprise had its birth in Christian cosmology. Science and Christianity do not just co-exist: they support each other. Christian cosmology teaches us that the universe was created by the supreme intelligence of God to function in accordance with the laws which he designed for it. These laws are rational and coherent. Science helps us to understand them. There is no danger that science is going to 'push God out' of the universe: on the contrary every new discovery only confirms the truth of revelation.

In this respect it becomes clear that the attack on science must have as one of its (perhaps unintended) consequences the undermining of Christianity itself. Because Christianity is so profoundly rooted in reality, and because the doctrine of the Incarnation makes it quite clear

43

Robert Whelan

to us that matter and spirit are indissolubly linked in the quest for eternal salvation, any creed or philosophy which turns people away from reality must also blind them to the author of that reality. The adherence to Christianity must decrease as interest in crystals, aromatherapy, tarot cards and horoscopes increases.

Perhaps nothing illustrates more completely the essentially religious nature of the Green movement than this desire to turn away from facts and reject the 'paradigm' of science when the hard-edged reality of the universe does not square with what we would like it to be. To find that you have been placing your faith in foolish things, whether they be witch doctors or global warming, is unsettling. The most comfortable response is to ignore the evidence and preserve your faith. David Brower, founder of Friends of the Earth in the USA, dismissed any questioning of environmentalists' claims by saying that 'the figures in themselves are merely indices. What matters is that they *feel* right',[98] while William Thompson, founder of the Lindisfarne Association in Scotland, claims that 'science fact is really a disguised form of science fiction'.[99] According to Brian Swimme and Thomas Berry, writing in *The Amicus Journal*, our traditional understanding of science will not be able to save the earth. This will require a 'return to the mythic origins of the scientific venture ... [This will] bring us deep into the realm of imaginative vision where we feel the scientist must participate to some extent in shamanic powers'.[100] In his book *Saviors of the Earth?* Michael Coffman notes that *The Amicus Journal* is published by the National Resources Defence Council (NRDC):

It was the NRDC ... that perpetrated the Alar scare. If it was shamanic powers which revealed to the leadership within the NRDC that Alar was poisoning America's children, then we have truly entered the twilight zone ... Are we to depend upon shamans to provide medical science, agricultural science, atmospheric science? ... Could shamanism have found the cure for polio? For tuberculosis, smallpox and other major killers?[101]

When the mumbo-jumbo of voodoo and shamanism is being described as part of 'the scientific venture', then clearly the very concept of scientific inquiry has been drained of any meaning. Climatologist Richard Lindzen of the Massachussetts Institute of Technology has

44

given a worrying account of the way in which the hysterical campaign to promote fear of global warming was conducted in the absence of any persuasive scientific evidence. He was the only scientist on the panel at a global warming symposium at Tufts University at which Claudine Schneider (then congresswoman for Rhode Island) announced: 'Scientists may disagree, but we can hear Mother Earth and she is crying'.[102] Truly, the sleep of reason brings forth monsters.

Pollution of the Sanctuary

Of course, when we speak of the attack on science we know that we are speaking of an attack which is doomed to failure. Science is not going to go away. In the West we have come to take it for granted that our standard of living will constantly be improving. This depends upon the application of science through technology. We will not give this up, whatever people may be telling opinion polls about the need to protect the environment.

That is not to say, however, that concerns about some uses of science are without foundation. Procedures such as gene-mapping, *in vitro* fertilisation including cross-species fertilisation, and the creation of babies for infertile couples from the eggs of aborted female fetuses raise the spectre of science as Frankenstein's monster rather than our useful servant. Such procedures, as well as others, fail to respect the dignity of the human person, and indeed seek to reduce the human person to the level of matter to be manipulated.

As we have seen above, Stanley Jaki and others have demonstrated that the matrix of a sustainable scientific culture lay in Christianity. Other cultures of the ancient world produced scientists who made discoveries which were of great significance in themselves, but they did not develop into a self sustaining scientific enterprise. The Christian doctrine of creation out of nothing and in time (*creatio ex nihilo et cum tempore*) gave scientific research the push that was needed to set it rolling down the hill. However, that is not to say that all scientific endeavour reflects the moral teaching of the church. Science itself is neither moral nor immoral: it is neutral. The moral dimension, governing the sort of research which is deemed ethical and the uses to which research may be put, must be supplied by human beings, the only creatures in God's creation endowed with a moral sense.

It is perhaps needless to observe that science slipped the leash, in

45

this respect, many years ago. Although almost all of the great scientists, from Galileo and Newton to Faraday and Einstein, were devout Christians, and although surveys have shown that about half of all scientists today still hold religious views, there is little doubt that scientific research is now carried out in an atmosphere which is devoid of ethical restraints, either Christian or otherwise. Hence the legitimate fear of science, on which Green extremists have been able to capitalise.

The situation has been aggravated by the uneasy feeling, which so many Christians seem to have inherited from the last century, that there is some conflict between science and religion, and that the less they know about it the better. People who have no direct experience of science, and who have given the matter little thought, will assume that Christians had better steer clear of scientific debate in case their faith is undermined.

This is not a view which would have appealed to Christians in earlier times. As Hanbury Brown wrote in his book *The Wisdom of Science*:

> Over the west door of Chartres Cathedral are the images of four great scientists (Euclid, Pythagoras, Ptolemy and Aristotle) together with Christ and the Saints. They were put there in the 12th century as an expression of the unity of science and religion. Can the Christian church, eight centuries later, recapture that vision?[103]

A.N. Whitehead put it even more strongly in *Science and the Modern World*:

> When we consider what religion is for mankind, and what science is, it is no exaggeration to say that the future course of history depends upon the decision of this generation as to the relations between them.[104]

Groundless Fears

As Jaki and others have shown, there is no need for Christians to fear science as Christianity is a faith grounded in reality. Scientific research, including the latest theories concerning the creation of the universe, cannot shake or undermine it. This is also true of environmental science.

One of the most frequently stated observations of present day environmentalists is that science has shown us that all organisms in the world are interconnected. We all affect and are affected by other parts of the creation. For this reason the 'ecosystem' or the 'biosphere' has to be considered as a whole.

The most famous exponent of this view is James Lovelock, an independent scientist and Fellow of the Royal Society, who devised what became known as the Gaia hypothesis. This states that, not only is all matter inter-connected, but that this network has some sort of intelligence which regulates the planet:

> ... the entire range of living matter on Earth, from whales to viruses, and from oaks to algae, could be regarded as constituting a single living entity, capable of manipulating the Earth's atmosphere to suit its overall needs and endowed with faculties and powers far beyond those of its constituent parts.[105]

Gaia was the name of the ancient Greek goddess of the earth, and Lovelock's hypothesis has been used by those who want to revive Earth Worship and particularly Goddess Worship. Lovelock has protested that he did not intend this, that he did not claim Gaia was sentient, and that he only refers to Gaia as 'she' in the same sense that a ship is referred to as 'she'.[106] However, it is not hard to see how some people have taken his Gaia hypothesis as the basis of a religious creed.

Lovelock marshals an impressive array of arguments to support his theory that:

> The climate and the chemical properties of the Earth now and throughout its history seem always to have been optimal for life. For this to have happened by chance is as unlikely as to survive unscathed a drive blindfold through rush-hour traffic.[107]

Perhaps the most remarkable of Lovelock's revelations is that, in the three and a half aeons of life on earth, the sun's output of energy has increased by 30 percent. In spite of this, the temperature on earth has never varied by more than one or two degrees. Some complex and scarcely understood mechanism has kept conditions on earth just right for the survival of life, neither too hot nor too cold.

Scarcely less wonderful is the composition of the atmosphere, another vital pre-condition for life, which Lovelock describes as:

> ... packed with a curious mixture of reactive gases forever in flux and chemical disarray yet never losing their balance ... the composition of the Earth's atmosphere was so curious and incompatible a mixture that it could not possibly have arisen or persisted by chance. Almost everything about it seemed to violate the rules of equilibrium chemistry, yet amidst apparent disorder relatively constant and favourable conditions for life were somehow maintained.[108]

Lovelock gives other wonderful examples of this balance which has enabled life to persist on earth. For example, the continuation of life in the seas depends upon a certain level of salinity: there must be not too much salt and not too little. We know that the salinity of the sea has varied very little in hundreds of millions of years, in spite of the fact that the run-offs of salt from rivers, rain and other sources should by now have made it much more salty than it is. So where is the sink in the sea? What mechanism keep that salinity at just the right level?

To the Christian reader of Lovelock's book it must seem that the answer to all of these questions is staring him in the face. The universe was created by God who sustains it in existence at every moment. This is the intelligence which directs and controls, not 'Gaia' or 'the biosphere'.

Lovelock's Gaia books are, quite incidentally, the final refutation of the heresy of Deism, so popular in the eighteenth century, which might crudely be described as the belief that the universe is like a great clock which God wound up at the beginning of time and then left to run. It is quite clear that the mechanisms of creation must have required constant fine-tuning in order to enable life to continue. From that we can deduce that the Intelligence which guides the universe must be present and active at all times.

Conclusion

This chapter has attempted to set out some of the reasons for which Christians might want to give the Green movement a wide berth, but this is not the same as saying that Christians should not be concerned about the state of the environment. As we know from the Book of Genesis, God created everything in the universe and he saw that it was good (Gen.1:1-25). We can come to know God through the beauty and wonder of his creation (Wisdom 13:1-9) and can in some measure respond to his love for us by caring for it.

However, the Christian approach to environmental problems must be based on the insights of the Christian faith, and must not mimic or repeat attitudes and beliefs which clearly come from a different spiritual perspective.

Christian Greens sometimes seem reluctant to confront the most important cause of environmental devastation mentioned in scripture, which is sin. Sin is the ultimate pollution, the dislocation of the relationship between ourselves and the Creator, which led to the expulsion from the Garden of Eden. The prophet Hosea blamed the sinfulness of the the Israelites for what we would now describe as the threat to biological diversity:

> ... there is no fidelity, no tenderness,
> no knowledge of God in the country ...
> This is why the country is in mourning,
> and all who live in it pine away,
> even the wild animals and the birds of heaven;
> the fish of the sea themselves are perishing.
>   Hos.4:2-3.

Christians who join with secular campaigners in attributing all environmental problems to technology or to political and economic systems are missing the point: they should be encouraging their fellow citizens to spend a bit more time looking into their hearts, and a bit less peering up their car exhausts.

In the Spring of 1993 the Competitive Enterprise Institute in Washington held a seminar on Ecology and Religion at which speakers from different Christian denominations addressed the question of how Christians should respond to the challenge of environmentalism. Peter Leithart, a Presbyterian pastor from Alabama, shared the important insight that references to pollution in the Bible never concern man's mistreatment of what we would call the ecosystem: they invariably refer to either moral or ritual pollution.

> ... the most dangerous form of pollution is pollution of God's sanctuary, which in the New Testament is the Christian Church. When the

49

Church and the world are filled with sin and idolatry, God intervenes in judgement, and His judgement often takes the form of an environmental catastrophe. God devastated the environment around the wicked cities of Sodom and Gomorrah (Genesis 19) ... God's judgement against Israel turned the Edenic land into a wilderness (Joel 2:3). Similarly, God destroyed the world and all living creatures in the flood, saving only eight people and representatives of each animal species. Ten plagues left Egypt ravaged. In each case, the Lord Himself wasted the environment as punishment for sin. This means that if we face real environmental catastrophes, our first response should be to turn to God in repentance and humility, pleading for His mercy. The fear of the Lord is the beginning of wise environmental policy.[109]

This is a warning which Christians would do well to heed. Fear of an environmental 'crisis' has been used to introduce into Christian churches forms of worship which the Bible condemns, including the worship of other gods, and liturgies celebrating inanimate nature. The acceptance of New Age teaching and rituals by many who describe themselves as Christians, and even by ministers of the Gospel, is also often due to concern for the environment.

Christians, and in particular church leaders, need to think hard about what it is that we mean by a good environment, and what Christians are called upon to do in pursuit of that goal. If we allow the church to drift further into forms of worship which are an abomination to the God of Abraham, Isaac and Jacob, then we may call down upon ourselves the curse which the Lord spoke to Jeremiah:

> I will requite their guilt and their sin twice over, since they have polluted my land with the corpses of their Horrors, and filled my heritage with their Abominations.
>
> Jer.16:18.

It would be worse than any hole in the ozone layer.

NOTES

1.   See Anna Bramwell, *Ecology in the 20th Century: A History*, New Haven: Yale University Press (1989) p.199, quoted in Doug Bandow, 'Ecol-

ogy as Religion: Faith in Place of Fact', *Proceedings from the Seminar on Ecology and Religion*, Competitive Enterprise Institute: Washington (1993) p. 24.

2. Reported in the *Journal of the American Medical Association* (30 September 1933) p. 1087.

3. For the Nazi cult of holistic medicine see Robert Proctor, *Racial Hygiene; Medicine under the Nazis*, Cambridge, MA: Harvard University Press (1988) p. 223 ff.

4. Al Gore, *Earth in the Balance*, New York: Penguin (1993) pp. 269 and 293.

5. Quoted in P. Johnson, 'The Earth Summit', *The United Nations Conference on Environment and Development (UNCED)*, London: Graham and Trotman/ Martinus Nijhoff (1993) p. 32.

6. Al Gore, op. cit., pp. 16 and 269.

7. Thomas Berry, *The Dream of the Earth*, San Francisco: Sierra Book Club (1990) p. 65.

8. Norman Myers and Julian Simon, *Scarcity or Abundance: A Debate on the Environment*, New York: W.W. Norton (1994) p. 107.

9. Jonathon Porritt and David Winner, *The Coming of the Greens*, London: Fontana (1988) pp. 193, 254, 233.

10. Maurice Strong, Statement at the opening of UNCED (3 June 1992). Printed and distributed at Rio de Janeiro. Quoted in Dixy Lee Ray and Lou Guzzo, *Environmental Overkill: Whatever Happened to Common Sense?* Washington: Regenery Gateway, 1993, p. 4

11. Bryan Appleyard, *Understanding the Present: Science and the soul of modern man*, London: Picador (1992) p. 134.

12. Willis B. Glover, *Biblical Origins of Modern Secular Culture: An Essay in the Interpretation of Western History*, Macon, GA: Mercer University Press (1984) p. 150. Quoted in Robert H. Nelson, 'Environmental Calvinism: The Judeo-Christian Roots of Eco-Theology' in Roger E.Meiners and Bruce Yandle (eds.) *Taking the Environment Seriously*, Lanham, Maryland: Rowan and Littlefield (1993) pp. 233-255.

13. Gustave Le Bon, *The Crowd: A Study of the Popular Mind*, New York: The Viking Press (1960), p. 73, quoted in Jo Kwong, 'Environmentalism: Ethics and Stewardship', paper given at the FEE Theological Conference (15-19 July 1991).

14. Warren Newman, *Environmentalism as Religion*, Political Notes No. 73, London: Libertarian Alliance (1992).

15. Doug Bandow, 'Ecology as Religion: Faith in Place of Fact', *Proceed-*

ings from the Seminar on Ecology and Religion, Washington: Competitive Enterprise Institute (1993) p. 26.

16. Robert H. Nelson, op.cit., p. 245.

17. Dan Sholly, defence minister of Yellowstone Nation, quoted in Micah Morrison, *Fire in Paradise: The Yellowstone Fires and the Politics of Environmentalism*, New York: HarperCollins (1993) p. 6.

18. Ibid., p. 65 ff.

19. *National Journal* (13 August 1988) pp.2095-6, quoted in Robert James Bidinotto, 'Environmentalism: Freedom's Foe for the 90s', *The Freeman* (November 1990), p. 418.

20. Gro Harlem Bruntland, 'The Test of Our Civilization', *New Perspectives Quarterly*, Vol 6 No 1 (Spring 1989) p. 5, quoted in Michael S. Coffman, *Saviors of the Earth?*, Chicago: Northfield Publishing (1994) p. 189.

21. Robert H. Nelson, 'Unoriginal Sin: The Judeo-Christian Roots of Ecotheology', *Policy Review* 53 (Summer) pp. 52-59.

22. Al Gore, op. cit., p. 12.

23. Ibid., p. 366.

24. Ibid., p. 88.

25. Ibid., p. 367.

26. Ibid., p. 297.

27. Ibid., p. 326.

28. Lynn White Jr., 'The Historic Roots of Our Ecologic Crisis', *Science*, Vol.155 No. 3767 (10 March 1967) pp. 1203-7.

29. Ibid, p. 1205

30. Ibid.

31. Ibid., p. 1207.

32. Ibid., p. 1205.

33. S. L. Jaki, 'The Last Century of Science: Progress, Problems and Prospects', *Proceedings of the Second International Humanistic Symposium*, Athens: Hellenistic Society for Humanistic Studies (1973) p. 259; See also Chapters 1-6 and Chapter 9 of S.L. Jaki, *Science and Creation: From Eternal Cycles to an Oscillating Universe*, Edinburgh: Scottish Academic Press (1974).

34. See Stanley L. Jaki, *Cosmos and Creator*, Edinburgh: Scottish Academic Press (1980) p. 77 and *passim*.

35. Paul Haffner, *Creation and Scientific Creativity: A Study in the Thought of S.L. Jaki*, Front Royal: Christendom Press (1991) p. 35.

36. Ibid., p. 37.

37. Lynn White Jr., op.cit., p. 1206.
38. Quoted in Stephen Fox, *John Muir and His Legacy: The American Conservation Movement*, Boston: Little Brown (1981) p. 5.
39. Henry David Thoreau, *The Natural History Essays*, Salt Lake City: Peregrine Smith (1980); quoted in Alston Chase, *Playing God in Yellowstone: The Destruction of America's First National Park*, Boston: The Atlantic Monthly Press (1986) p. 302.
40. Alston Chase, op.cit., p. 301.
41. Stephen Fox, op.cit, quoted in Alston Chase, op.cit., p. 302.
42. Richard D. North, quoted in Jonathon Porritt and David Winner, *The Coming of the Greens*, London: Fontana (1988) pp. 251-2.
43 Bill McKibben, *The End of Nature*, New York: Random House (1989), quoted in Robert H. Nelson, 'Unoriginal Sin: The Judeo-Christian Roots of Ecotheology', *Policy Review* 53 (Summer) pp. 52-59.
44 Robert H. Nelson, op.cit.
45. Randy England, *The Unicorn in the Sanctuary: The Impact of the New Age on the Catholic Church*, Rockford, Illinois: Tan Books, (1991).
46. Constance Cumbey, *The Hidden Dangers of the Rainbow: The New Age Movement and Our Coming Age of Barbarism*, Lafayette LA: Huntington House (1983)
47. Michel Rocard, press release (in typescript) issued at Rio, (June 1992), quoted in Dixy Lee Ray with Lou Guzzo, *Environmental Overkill: Whatever Happened to Common Sense?*, Washington: Regnery Gateway (1993) p. 10-11.
48. see Dixy Lee Ray with Lou Guzzo, op.cit., pp. 85-88.
49. Christopher Manes, *Green Rage: Radical Environmentalism and the Unmaking of Civilisation*, Boston: Little Brown (1990) p. 232.
50. Ibid., p. 237.
51. Ibid., p. 166, quoting Mike Roselle, 'Deep Ecology and the New Civil Rights Movement', *Earth First!* (1 May 1988) p. 23.
52. Ibid., p. 141, citing Lynton Caldwell, *International Environmental Policy: Emergence and Dimensions*, Durham, North Carolina: Duke University Press (1984).
53. Rupert Sheldrake *The Rebirth of Nature: The Greening of Science and God*, New York: Bantam Books (1991) p. 223, quoted in Doug Bandow, 'Ecology as Religion: Faith in Place of Fact', *Proceedings from the Seminar on Ecology and Religion*, Washington: Competitive Enterprise Institute (1993) p. 19.
54. Jeremy Rifkin and Ted Howard, *Entropy: Into the Greenhouse World*,

New York: Bantam Books, (1989) p. 266, quoted in Doug Bandow, op.cit., p. 19.

55. James Nash, *Loving Nature: Ecological Integrity and Christian Responsibility*, Nashville: Abingdon Press: (1991) p. 19, quoted in Doug Bandow, op.cit., p. 19.

56. Thomas Berry C.P. with Thomas Clarke S.J., *Befriending the Earth: A Theology of Reconciliation between humans and the earth*, Mystic Connecticut: Twenty-Third Publications, (1991) p. 120-1.

57. Chris Seaton, *Whose Earth?*, Shelford, Cambridge: Crossway Books (1992) p. 154.

58. Jeremy Rifkin, *Biosphere Politics; A New Consciousness for a New Century*, New York: Crown Publishers Inc. (1991) p. 273.

59. Matthew Fox, *Original Blessing*, Santa Fe, New Mexico: Bear and Company (1983) p. 55.

60. Ibid., p. 9.

61. Ibid., p. 26.

62. Ibid., p. 119 and p. 183.

63. Thomas Berry C.P. with Thomas Clarke S.J., op.cit., p. 81.

64. Ibid., p. 6.

65 Ibid., p. 96.

66. Ibid. pp. 47-8.

67. Ibid., p. 76.

68. Ibid., p. 21.

69. *The Assisi Declarations: Messages on Man & Nature from Buddhism, Christianity, Hinduism, Islam and Judaism*, World Wide Fund for Nature, 29 September 1986.

70. Martin Palmer, Anne Nash, Ivan Hattingh (eds.) *Faith and Nature*, Century Hutchinson/WWF, undated, p. 56.

71. "Religion and Nature Interfaith Ceremony", WWF (1986).

72. "Canterbury Festival of Faith and the Environment", promotional leaflet published by WWF (1989).

73. From 'Run Away', a song from *Yanomamo: An Ecological Musical*, music by Peter Rose, words by Anne Conlon, published by Joseph Weinberger Ltd in association with the World Wide Fund for Nature (1988) p. 19.

74. Letter, *The Church Times* (29 September 1989).

75. *Faith and the Environment*, leaflet published by WWF, UK.

76. Leyla Alyanak, 'Seeds of Change: The New Harvest', *The New Road*, Bulletin of the WWF Network on Conservation and Religion, Issue 4

(Jan-March 1988)

77. *Creation Festival Liturgy*, WWF/ICOREC (1988) p.24.

78. Walter Schwartz, 'Building a church for Gaia', *The Guardian* (5 September 1992).

79. Elizabeth Breuilly and Martin Palmer, *Christianity and Ecology*, London: Cassell (1992).

80. Matthew Hale, *The Primitive Origination of Mankind*, London (1677) p. 370. Quoted in Ian Bradley, *God is Green*, London: Darton, Longman & Todd (1990) p. 91.

81. Ian Bradley, op. cit., p. 107

82. Ibid., p. 58.

83. Ibid., p. 97.

84. Ibid., p. 105.

85. *Forest Resources Assessment 1990: Tropical Countries*, FAO Forestry Paper 112, Rome: United Nations Food and Agriculture Organisation (1993) p. 24.

86. Jonathon Porritt, 'Seeing Green: How we can create a more satisfying society', *Utne Reader*, Minneapolis: Lens Publishing Co (Nov-Dec 1989) p. 77. Taken from an article originally published in *One Earth* (Winter 1988), the journal of the Findhorn Foundation.

87. George Wuerthner, 'Tree Spiking and Moral Maturity', *Earth First!* (1 August 1985) p. 20; quoted in Christopher Manes, op.cit., p. 176.

88. Lynn White Jr., op.cit., p. 1206.

89. Thomas Berry O.P. with Thomas Clarke S.J., op.cit., pp. 19 and 21.

90. Sean McDonagh, *The Greening of the Church*, London: Geoffrey Chapman (1990) p. 96-7.

91. Edward Goldsmith, *The Way: An Ecological World View*, London: Rider, (1992) p. 64.

92. Ibid., pp. 188 and 364.

93. Ibid., pp. 80 and 81.

94. Ibid., pp. 377 and 378.

95. Bryan Appleyard, op. cit., pp. 149 and 7.

96. Ibid., p. 108.

97. Ibid., p. 8-9.

98. Quoted by Michael S. Coffman in *Saviors of the Earth?*, Chicago: Northfield Publishing (1994) p. 87.

99. Ibid., p. 88, Quoting from a Lindisfarne Association newsletter, January 1992.

100. Brian Swimme and Thomas Berry, 'The Universe Story: A New, Cel-

ebratory Cosmology', *The Amicus Journal* (Winter 1993) pp. 30-31.

101. Michael S. Coffman, op.cit., p. 87.

102. Richard S. Lindzen, 'Global Warming: The Origin of Consensus' in John A. Baden (ed.) *Environmental Gore: A Constructive Response to "Earth in the Balance"*, San Francisco: Pacific Research Institute (1995) p. 127.

103. Hanbury Brown, *The Wisdom of Science*, Cambridge University Press (1986) p. 184, quoted in Roger Nesbitt, *The Path From Science to God*, Wallington, Surrey: Faith Keyway Trust p. 9.

104. A.N. Whitehead, *Science and the Modern World*, Cambridge University Press (1932) p. 224, quoted in Roger Nesbitt, op.cit., p. 9.

105. J.E. Lovelock, *Gaia: A New Look At Life on Earth*, Oxford: Oxford University Press (1987) p. 9.

106. Ibid., p. xii.

107. Ibid., p. 10.

108. Ibid., pp. 65, 67 and 69.

109. Peter J. Leithart, 'Snakes in the Garden: Sanctuaries, Sanctuary Pollution and the Global Environment' in *Proceedings from the Seminar on Ecology and Religion, April 30 - May 1 1993*, Washington: Competitive Enterprise Institute (1993) p. 67.

CHAPTER TWO
Greens and People

Robert Whelan

In searching for a new enemy to unite us, we came up with the idea that pollution, the threat of global warming, water shortages, famine and the like would fit the bill ... All these dangers are caused by human intervention ... The real enemy, then, is humanity itself.

The Club of Rome, 1991[1]

The Birth of Greenery

Care for the environment is nothing new. Human beings have been striving to improve their surroundings ever since the start of human settlements. When the basic needs for food, warmth and shelter have been met, then it is time to start tidying up the place.

Nor is the advent of campaigning pressure groups for environmental causes particularly new. Some, like the National Trust, the Society for the Protection of Ancient Buildings and the Royal Society for the Prevention of Cruelty to Animals can point to histories of a century and more. Even in its more modern manifestation, as the scourge of industrial society and the advocate of back-to-nature simplicity, we must date the environmental movement from at least the publication of Rachel Carson's book *Silent Spring* in 1962.[2]

However, developments in the 1980s put a completely new slant on things. By a strange sort of political osmosis, a number of pressure group causes which had previously functioned separately came together to make common cause. The Green movement as we now know it represents an amalgam of vegetarians, animal rights activists, wildlife and heritage lobbyists, organic food faddists, anti-nuclear campaigners, advocates of holistic medicine and 'alternative lifestyles' and other interest groups.

These groups had previously functioned independently, running

57

their own campaigns and enjoying their several successes. However, as a united movement, they proved to be more than the sum of their parts. Western culture seemed to turn green, if not overnight, then certainly within a very short space of time. The Ecology Party in Britain changed its name to the Green Party in 1985, and all other political parties began to vie with each other to be the greenest, including the National Front! In 1985 Margaret Thatcher had classed the Greens together with communists as part of 'the enemy within'. Three years later she made a speech to the Royal Society committing her government to a green agenda, and Lady Thatcher was not noted for her U-turns.

Large numbers of people were persuaded that Western lifestyles were 'unsustainable', and that a radical change was needed in everything from the economy to transport and shopping habits. For the constituent parts of the Green movement, unity had indeed proved to be strength. People who, for many years, had been regarded as harmless but cranky individuals were suddenly invited to give advice to the leaders of society. Views which had recently been regarded as the height of eccentricity were at the centre of political debate.

The chance to join a broader movement came as a lifeline for some of the groups concerned. For example, the lobby for nuclear disarmament had declined from being *the* popular cause for mass protest of the 1970s to being virtually invisible as a result of *glasnost* and the ending of the cold war.

There was another important element in this blend of pressure group causes which was to have a profound effect on the policies and attitudes of Greenery: the population control movement.

Stop Those People!

The population controllers had been arguing since the 1950s that global population growth would usher in every imaginable economic and social evil, and that wars, poverty and famine would increase until this Pandora's box could be shut by the universal provision of birth control to ensure small families, especially in the Third World.

The idea that virtually every problem in the world came down to overpopulation proved to be so easy to promote that it quickly became established as part of the popular orthodoxy. Overpopulation was regarded as a fact — one of those things that 'everyone knows'.

However, a strange thing happened. As the years went by global population increased more rapidly than at any time in history, doubling between the 1950s and the 1980s from approximately 2.5 billion to over 5 billion. In spite of this, the day of doom did not arrive: none of the terrifying forecasts of the effects of population growth came true.

The first scare story, on the back of which the population control movement had been launched, was the prospect of famines. It was regarded as self-evident that the world's population would outgrow the capacity of the earth to feed us all. However the food supply proved not only equal to keeping up with the greatest increase in global population in history: it kept way ahead.

Per capita food production — that is, the amount of food available for each person in the world if it were all divided equally — is constantly reaching record levels. In the 1950s and 1960s agricultural economists used to try to calculate the maximum population which the world could feed. They reached such astronomical figures — 30 to 50 billion, against a present world population of less than 6 billion — that the calculations were abandoned as being of no relevance. We live now in a world of gross food surpluses in which Western farmers are paid millions of pounds annually *not to produce food*, for fear of glutting world markets completely.

The next big scare was that natural resources would run out. In 1972 the Club of Rome published its famous report *The Limits to Growth*, predicting the exhaustion of natural resources. By dividing known reserves by consumption, the report gave dates by which major resources would be finished. The exhaustion of known reserves of certain resources, assuming exponential growth in demand, was predicted as follows: Gold 1981; Mercury 1985; Silver 1985; Tin 1987; Petroleum 1992; Copper 1993; Lead 1993; Natural gas 1994. Assuming total reserves to be five times the known reserves in 1972, and allowing for exponential growth in demand, the dates moved on as follows: Gold 2001; Mercury 2013; Silver 2014; Copper 2020; Natural gas 2021; Petroleum 2022; Tin 2033; Lead 2036.[3] No one would take these estimates seriously now. As Harvard economist Robert Stavins put it in an assessment of the Club of Rome's track record: 'reserves have increased; demand has changed; substitution has occurred; and recycling has been stimulated'.[4] The predictions were made on the basis of simplistic assumptions fed into a computer model which were described by Fred Pearce, news editor of *New Scientist*, as 'more the stuff of computer games than science ... Galactic invaders in arcade games have obliterated the Earth on the basis of more sophisticated analysis'.[5] The world is now richer in resources than ever before and the advent of new technology has made us less and less dependent on physical resources. For example, the silicone for silicone chips is found in sand, to which there is no realistic limit.

Empirical evidence also made nonsense of the notion that population growth causes poverty. Countries like Japan, Hong Kong, Taiwan, South Korea and Singapore experienced spectacular economic growth concurrent with rapid population growth, which gave them some of the highest population densities in the world. Even the President of the World Bank, a body committed for many years to reducing population growth, was forced to tell a gathering of the International Planned Parenthood Federation:

> The evidence is clear that economic growth rates in excess of population growth rates can be achieved and maintained, by both developed and developing countries.[6]

Where Now?

By the beginning of the 1980s the *rationale* for population control was beginning to wear thin. However by this time the population control movement was a multi-billion dollar industry, employing tens of thousands of population planners, and financed largely by Western taxpayers' money. In order to remain in funds, the population controllers had to find new arguments on which to base their programmes.

At this critical moment, the Green bandwagon started to roll downhill. It proved to be the salvation of the population lobby because, if more human beings don't mean more poverty or famine or unemployment, they certainly do mean more human activity. If this activity could be shown to be, *of itself*, destructive and undesirable, then the population controllers would be back in business.

People as Pollution

In 1985 an umbrella organisation was formed in Britain called Common Ground International. Its aim was to bring together environmental organisations with population organisations on the pretext that, whilst they had in the past worked separately, their concerns were now so close together that it made sense to join forces.

Their first project was a touring exhibition called 'Let's Get It Together'. Aimed mainly at children, it comprised a series of panels blaming population growth for every imaginable horror, including child abuse. Visitors were greeted at the entrance to the exhibition by full length mirrors emblazoned with the legend YOU ARE LOOKING AT THE MOST DANGEROUS FORM OF LIFE ON EARTH. The children were, of course, looking at themselves.

This set the tone for the arguments for population control which we were to hear in the years ahead. In striving to make population into an environmental issue, the population lobbyists argued that the population explosion was *the* environmental problem, and that nothing would improve on the environmental front until it was dealt with.

This was the origin of the idea that people are a form of pollution, or *popullution*. Jonathon Porritt summarised the philosophy as 'living is polluting',[7] which is to say that anything we do will make the world a worse place.

Every environmental problem could then be put down to the nefarious activities of the ever-growing numbers of people. According to *The Gaia Atlas of Planet Management*:

> The rapidly manifesting global crises, the long shadow, cast by the fast-growing figure of humankind, is stretching into the very heart of our biosphere ... we should speak of a single over-arching crisis: the crisis of humankind. The shadow stems from all of us, and it will darken all our lives.[8]

The arguments for population control fell on fertile ground in the environmental movement. Green literature is shot through with the most negative images of the human race, which is compared to an infectious disease in *The Gaia Peace Atlas*,[9] and to a 'super-malignancy on the face of the planet' in *The Gaia Atlas of Planet Management*.[10] Human beings appear as 'a cancer on the rest of the biosphere'[11] to Fr. Sean McDonagh and as 'the affliction of the world' and 'its demonic presence' to Fr. Thomas Berry.[12] Stephen Hawking, author of the best-seller *A Brief History of Time*, describes the human race as 'chemical scum floating on the surface of the earth'[13] and Paul Watson, co-founder of Greenpeace in America, as 'the AIDS of the Earth'.[14] A recruiting leaflet produced by Greenpeace in the UK had this to say about the species of Man:

> Modern Man has made a rubbish tip of Paradise. He has multiplied his numbers to plague proportions, caused the extinction of 500 species of animals, ransacked the planet for fuels and now stands like a brutish infant, gloating over his meteoric rise to ascendancy, on the brink of a war to end all wars and of effectively destroying this oasis of life in the solar system.[15]

The cumulative effect of these revolting images of human beings is to de-sensitize the reader. When it has become possible to regard people of whom one personally disapproves as a low or degenerate form of life, then drastic solutions to deal with the 'problem' of other people seem acceptable.

In his book *The Intellectuals and the Masses* John Carey has shown that this tendency to dehumanise groups of people by the use of pejorative terms such as vermin, scum, swarming insects, spawn and so on, has an impressive intellectual pedigree. It was a commonplace amongst a number of leading figures in European culture at the end of the last century and the beginning of this, and Carey is able to illustrate his argument with quotations from Bernard Shaw, H.G. Wells, Virginia Woolf, E.M. Forster and many others. Carey attributes the revulsion felt by these people towards 'the masses' to the fear of the emerging popular culture of mass circulation newspapers, radio and cinema. The intellectuals were not in control of these mass media, and felt that their position as guardians of European culture was under threat. They therefore amused themselves by devising methods to exterminate the rabble. According to D.H. Lawrence:

> To learn plainly to hate mankind, to detest the spawning human being, that is the only cleanliness now [16] ... If I had my way, I would build a lethal chamber as big as the Crystal Palace.[17]

He was supported in his views by Bernard Shaw:

> ... if we desire a certain type of civilization and culture, we must exterminate the sort of people who do not fit into it.[18]

Carey points out that Hitler repeatedly referred to the Jews as a bacterial disease, and compared the campaign against them to the work of Pasteur and Koch (who discovered the TB vacillus). Hitler wrote in *Mein Kampf*:

> The discovery of the Jewish virus is one of the greatest revolutions the world has seen. The struggle in which we are now engaged is similar to the one waged by Pasteur and Koch in the last century. How many diseases must owe their origin to the Jewish virus![19]

As Carey points out, the dehumanising language paved the way for something much worse:

> Mass transportation, destruction and incineration [of Jews], and the mass production of fertilizer from their ashes, all acquired a certain appropriateness once the initial proposal that they were a mass — not fully alive people — was accepted.[20]

Just as the de-humanising language used to describe the Jews made the 'final solution' seem acceptable, so the images of human beings in Green literature as a 'horde of rats', an 'uncontrolled virus' and an 'infestation' on the planet predispose people towards accepting dramatic methods of population control.[21] The widespread support amongst Western intellectuals, who would regard themselves as liberal and humane, for the Chinese government's one-child-per-couple population control programme indicates the extent to which concern for human rights can be suspended in a 'good cause', like dealing with 'overpopulation'. The Chinese programme involves the harassment, punishment and even the forced abortion of women who dare to achieve 'unauthorised' pregnancies.[22] It is partly funded by Western taxpayers' money channelled through international agencies like the United Nations Population Fund. Although the Chinese programme is the most famously coercive population control initiative in the world, most population programmes are built around policies which interfere with the freedom of parents to decide on the number of children they wish to have. Population control literature is full of examples of propaganda campaigns, the manipulation of tax and welfare systems and the use of rewards and punishments to bring reproductive behaviour into line with predetermined guidelines laid down by national and international bureaucrats. The reproductive 'freedom' which population lobbyists speak of is the 'freedom' to have a small family, not a large one.[23]

'It Will End in Tears'

According to the Greens, nothing we do is right. They admit that food production has increased faster than population growth, but claim that we have poisoned the earth and the seas with chemicals to achieve this; they cannot deny that resources have become cheaper and more easily available, but pretend we are on the verge of exhausting supplies so that we will bequeath a bankrupt world to our descendants; and when confronted with the rapid progress made in some developing countries in matters such as health care, which is bringing life expectancy closer to Western levels, the Greens claim that this is all based on 'unsustainable lifestyles' which have brought Western civilisation to the point of collapse and will do the same for the Third World.

As the old saying goes, truly no good deed shall go unpunished. Many people have been persuaded that human beings are such a bad lot, it would be better for the planet if there were fewer of us — or even none at all. In 1989 the *Sunday Times* gave over a whole issue of its magazine section to environmental doom-mongering, carrying the headline THE WORLD IS DYING, and rammed the message home with the sub-heading YOU DAMAGE THE EARTH JUST BY LIVING ON IT.[24] Even *The Economist* could thunder in an editorial:

> The extinction of the human species may not only be inevitable, but a good thing ... That is not to say that the rise of human civilization is insignificant, but there is no way of showing that it will be much help to the world in the long run.[25]

How to Lose People

Against this background of anti-human prejudice it is easy to grasp the Greens' enthusiasm for population control programmes. At the extreme edge we hear calls for reductions in the human population almost amounting to extinction:

Massive human diebacks would be good. It is our duty to cause them. It is our species' duty, relative to the whole, to eliminate 90 percent of our numbers.[26]

Some have even welcomed AIDS as a means of achieving this,[27] while the newsletter of the radical Earth First! organisation called for research into a 'species specific virus' that would destroy mankind.[28] An article in *Wild Earth*, a magazine edited by Dave Foreman, cofounder of Earth First!, asked the reader to consider 'voluntary human extinction' on the grounds that:

> ... the extinction of Homo sapiens would mean survival for millions, if not billions, of Earth-dwelling species ... Phasing out the human race will solve every problem on earth, social and environmental.[29]

These views are by no means confined to flakey outposts of Green fanaticism. Prince Philip, the International President of the World Wide Fund for Nature (WWF) has expressed a wish 'for reincarnation as a particularly deadly virus' in order to deal with the population explosion,[30] while the British Green Party has called for a reduction of the UK population from the present 57 million to between 35-40 million.[31] Although Sara Parkin, one of the leaders of the Green Party, insisted that this would not involve coercion, it is difficult to imagine how else such a dramatic drop in numbers could be achieved. There is certainly no historical precedent for it.

It is also disquieting that the book *A Green Manifesto* by activists Sandy Irvine and Alec Ponton, which is recommended by Parkin in her book *Green Parties*,[32] advocates:

> ... payments for periods of non-pregnancy ... tax benefits for families with fewer than two children; sterilization bonuses; withdrawal of maternity and similar benefits after a second child; larger pensions for people with fewer than two children ... an end to infertility research and treatment; a more realistic approach to abortion.[33]

On the international front the authors claim that:

> ... help given to regimes opposed to population policies is counterproductive and should cease. They are the true enemies of life and do

not merit support. So too are those religions which do not actively support birth control. Green governments would reluctantly have to challenge head-on such damaging beliefs.[34]

Irvine and Ponton also quote approvingly American population guru Kingsley Davis who said:

> If having too many children were considered as great a crime against humanity as murder, rape and thievery, we would have no qualms about 'taking freedom away'.[35]

This sort of rhetoric does not encourage readers to put too much trust in Green claims that population reduction will be achieved without coercion.

Are People Really So Bad?

As we have already said, the Green commitment to population control grows out of their view of human beings as, in Anita Roddick's phrase, 'the agents of destruction'.[36] If it were true this would constitute a strong argument for limiting human numbers. However we have to ask, where is the evidence that people are intrinsically destructive, and that population growth degrades the environment?

Of course human beings can be destructive, but they can also be constructive. They sometimes act from selfish motives, but they can also be altruistic, caring and positive. Human care and attention can turn a swamp into a park; a stream into a lake; a wilderness into a farm and a desert into a livable environment. All that is needed is the determination and the resources.

On one point we must agree with the Greens; human beings certainly do affect their environment. You can discern human settlements from the air by their straight lines and curves. We shape the natural world to make it fit our needs. Our human ingenuity enables us to create order out of chaos, and to plan, build and invest for the future in a way which would be impossible for even the highest species of the brute creation.

This capacity for making the world comfortable is something of which human beings used to be proud, and of which they should still be proud. It reflects the wondrous gift of reason which the Creator gave to man alone amongst his creation. The almost complete domination which we have achieved over the rest of the natural order reflects our special position in creation. Unlike any other creature, we were made in God's image eventually to spend eternity with him. God gave to Adam complete command over the rest of the natural order, and he was even more explicit with Noah after the Flood:

> God blessed Noah and his sons, saying to them, 'Be fruitful, multiply and fill the earth. Be the terror and the dread of all the wild beasts and all the birds of heaven, of everything that crawls on the ground and all the fish of the sea; they are handed over to you'.
>
> Gen.9:1-2

As the Psalmist put it:

> The heavens belong to the Lord
> but the earth he has given to men.
> Ps.113b (115):16

However, according to a certain strand of Green thinking, human beings are a blight on the landscape. They want to litter it up with structures for living and working; they want to join settlements with roads and railways; they want to cut down trees to cultivate the land. The view that signs of human occupancy and activity are *of themselves* undesirable is now so widely accepted that any plans for major development must take into account the lengthy processes of enquiry and appeal which will be held to establish whether or not a particular housing estate or rail link can be allowed to 'spoil' the environment.

It is almost as if we feel embarrassed about being here at all. Peter Palumbo, the millionaire developer and one-time Chairman of the Arts Council of Great Britain, has built himself a house in the Hebrides which is completely underground because 'the islands are so beautiful it would be a great pity if the hand of man was to be seen'.[37]

In what amounts to a very remarkable reversal of traditional values, the Greens see human beings as most successful when they do the least. For example, an article praising tribal wisdom in *People and the Planet*, the magazine of the International Planned Parenthood Federation, had this to say of Amazonian Indians:

67

Such people walk lightly on the landscape, *with such success* that out-
siders often consider their habitats a 'wilderness', as if no people had
ever lived there (emphasis added).[38]

The same view was expressed by Edward Goldsmith, the founder of
The Ecologist, in his book *The Way*:

Ecologically the temporary settlements of nomads are the most desirable, because they have the smallest impact on the environment.[39]

He goes on to quote the anthropologist W. E. H. Stanner who claimed
that Australian Aborigines make less impact on the environment than
beavers, who build dams, and termites who build nests. If bugs are
now being held up to us as role models, then we have clearly come a
long way from the biblical view of man as the lord of creation!

A Loss of Confidence

In an important sense, the Green movement is the product of the massive loss of self-confidence which has characterised Western societies since the end of the Second World War. We appear to have lost
confidence in our values and our civilisation, and even in our Judaeo-
Christian religious tradition from which these spring. As the mainstream churches have lost numbers, and as religious education has
degenerated in many schools into little more than exhortations to 'be
caring', so many people have grown up without the answers to life's
most basic questions. They do not really know why they are here on
earth or what they are supposed to be doing. The Green movement
plays on this profound insecurity by telling them that anything they
do is wrong, and it would be better if they were to lay low. According
to *The Gaia Peace Atlas*:

Ecologists and green movements see human civilization as out of step
with Gaia, and thus unsustainable in both spiritual and material terms
... Within Gaia, every organism is linked ... but human kind grossly
interferes, threatening its continuity.[40]

This gloomy picture of humankind is not compatible with the Christian view of creation, and man's place in the natural order.

... what is man that you should keep him in mind,
   mortal man that you care for him?

Yet you have made him little less than a god;
   with glory and honour you crowned him,
gave him power over the works of your hand,
   put all things under his feet.

All of them, sheep and cattle,
   yes, even the savage beasts,
birds of the air, and fish
   that make their way through the waters.

                                              Ps.8:4-8

Christians believe that God made man in his own image, with an immortal soul, with the gift of reason and the gift of free will. Man is thus given the wonderful opportunity of responding to God's love in such a way as to gain eternal life with him. This option is not open to the animals, let alone vegetables and minerals.

The difficulties we now face in providing ourselves with the necessities of life contrast sadly with the blissful state in which our first parents lived in the Garden of Eden, but they are not insuperable. By exercising our gifts we can cultivate the land, manufacture goods to meet our needs, and organise our societies along lines which reflect a love of justice and compassion. This is what we are intended to do. It is part of God's plan for us as we work out our salvation in this world, in preparation for eternity with him in the next.

The idea that, in so doing, we could possibly be disturbing 'Gaia', or infringing the territory of other species, is not one which the Christian mind can easily entertain. Jesus Christ did not die on the cross for Gaia, or for the wetlands, or for the rain forests, but for us.

It is clear that calls for population control are based on a reductionist view of man which is incompatible with Christian teaching. It is distressing to note how omnipresent this downgrading of human beings in relation to other species has become in Green thought and literature. For example Dr. M.S. Swaminathan, outgoing President of the International Union for the Conservation of Nature, claimed that:

Unless the penguin and the poor evoke from us equal concern, conservation will be a lost cause.[41]

French actress Brigitte Bardot believes that 'whoever feels compassion for an old man or a baby will feel the same for an animal and vice-versa',[42] while the obverse of that argument is put by Carla Lane, the successful creator of TV sitcoms like *Bread*:

If you harm an animal you might as well harm a child. There's no difference whatsoever.[43]

The same attitude was reflected in the defence put forward by a member of the Animal Liberation Front for the car bomb which critically injured a 13-month old baby: 'Cruelty to children is no worse than cruelty to animals'.[44]

Down with People

This view of human beings amounts to a downgrading which puts them not just on the same level as the animals but in some ways beneath them, because humans are supposed to have been so destructive. The growth of human populations is deplored because it is squeezing out the wild animals. According to James Lovelock, inventor of the Gaia hypothesis:

The real pollution is people. There's something like 5 billion people in the world and its increasing all the time. And this means that we are denying to Gaia a significant fraction of the land's surface ... I value life more than I value human beings.[45]

The Green, or Gaian, philosophy has its own view of the end of the human race, which it sees as an inevitable result of human pollution. According to Lovelock:

If we think only of ourselves and degrade the earth, then it will respond by replacing humans with a more amenable species ... I think we should see ourselves as members of a very democratic planetary community and remember that, in a democracy, we can be voted out.[46]

This is a view which is shared by Prince Philip. In his Presidential Address to members of the Royal Society of Arts in 1988 he painted a picture of the human race wiping itself off the face of the planet by its own polluting activities. The world would then go on turning without us.[47]

Once again, we have to say that although these views may be intriguing, they have nothing to do with Christian teaching. Gaia did not create man, and will not end his spell on earth. To suggest that pollution will bring the world, or man's time in it, to an end is to deny God the sovereignty over his own creation. The Christian teaching is that Jesus Christ will come again in glory at the end of time to redeem his creation. When this will be we cannot know (Mark 13:32-37; Acts 1:7) but it will be in God's time and not dependent on global warming or cutting down trees.

The downgrading of human beings and the elevation of animals is more than an intellectual exercise. It has had profound consequences for the well-being of two groups of people whose needs we shall now consider: the unborn and the citizens of less developed countries.

Greens and Abortion

We have witnessed, throughout the last twenty years, a growing movement to establish legally-enforceable 'rights' for animals. Throughout the Western world a plethora of laws has been passed to protect whales, seals, birds of prey, spotted owls and natterjack toads. There is scarcely any animal or insect species which has not found its constituency of human supporters. International agreements, often reached as a result of massive media coverage featuring dramatic pictures of bleeding animal corpses, have severely restricted the hunting of seals and whales. The lobby for an international ban on the ivory trade has been successful, in spite of the fact that countries which permit the trade such as Zimbabwe and South Africa have increased their herds of elephants considerably,[48] and the fur trade in Britain is on the verge of extinction due to animal rights activists. Those who disturb colonies of bats or the nests of the condor eagle can face stiff fines and even prison sentences.

At the same time abortion, which for hundreds of years was regarded as murder, has become widely accepted as a normal part of modern life. Despite the fact that advances in embryology and fetology have established beyond doubt that the baby in the womb is alive and human from the moment of conception, the Western nations have almost all taken steps to remove legal protection from the unborn. The child in the womb no longer enjoys the most basic of all human rights: the right to his or her own life.

Abortion has led to the acceptance of practices so barbaric that they would have been regarded as unthinkable only thirty years ago. These include the trade in human parts from aborted fetuses, the use of living human embryos for experimental purposes, the cannibalising of aborted babies for fetal material to'patch-up' adult patients suffering from conditions such as Parkinson's Disease, and even the use of eggs from aborted female fetuses to create new babies for infertile couples through *in vitro* fertilisation.

Is it a co-incidence that animal rights have increased as human rights have decreased, or are these two things linked? Are they, in fact, both part of the same equation, which involves a radical re-assessment of the value which we place on human beings in the order of creation?

Animal Rights and Human Wrongs

Oscar Wilde once noted that the love of animals which drives people to vegetarianism is sometimes counter-balanced by a dislike of people:

> It is strange that the most violent republicans I know are all vegetarians: Brussels sprouts seem to make people bloodthirsty, and those who live on lentils and artichokes are always calling for the gore of the aristocracy and for the severed heads of Kings.[49]

The same point has been made, less humorously, in our own time by Jim Mason and Peter Singer in *Animal Factories*:

> We who have an affinity with nonhuman animals and nature ... are finding it increasingly difficult to love our fellow 'man'.[50]

The inversion of normal human sympathies which characterises animal rights activists was mocked by Martin Morse Wooster in a review of environmental magazines for *Reason*.

While every other media outlet in the country condemned the murderous crimes of Deng Xiaoping and his henchmen, *The Animals' Agenda* reported the real story: The butchers of Beijing had slaughtered 12,000 dogs! ... The slaughter in Tiananmen Square, of course, was not reported.[51]

However, the irrational devotion to animals which blinds people to the sufferings of their fellow humans has a deadly serious aspect. The archetype of the animal lover/human hater was Adolf Hitler, whose strong ideological commitment to vegetarianism was emphasised by Nazi propaganda:

Do you know that your Fuhrer is a vegetarian, and that he does not eat meat because of his general attitude towards life and his love for the world of animals? ... Do you know that your Fuhrer is an ardent opponent of any torture of animals, in particular of vivisection? ... [Hitler will] fulfill his role as the saviour of animals from continuous and nameless torments and pain ... by making vivisection illegal.[52]

Hitler once chided a colleague who hunted:

How can you find any pleasure in shooting behind cover at poor creatures browsing on the edge of a wood, innocent, defenceless, and unsuspecting? Properly considered it's pure murder ... Nature is so marvellously beautiful and every animal has a right to live.[53]

The legal protection of animals had been one of the first policies to be implemented by the Nazis after gaining power. In 1933 Hermann Göring, head of the German Humane Society and Environmental Minister for the Third Reich, announced:

An absolute and permanent ban on vivisection is not only a necessary law to protect animals and to show sympathy with their pain, but it is also a law for humanity itself ... I have therefore announced the immediate prohibition of vivisection and have made the practice a punishable offence in Prussia. Until such time as punishment is pronounced the culprit shall be lodged in a concentration camp.[54]

This was no idle threat. Göring sent a fisherman to a concentration camp for cutting up a frog as bait. Truly, as Cyril Connolly said, love of animals is the honey of the misanthrope.

In their exposé of the animal rights movement *Animal Scam: The Beastly Abuse of Human Rights*, Kathleen Marquardt, Herbert Levine and Mark LaRochelle argue that the Nazis' elevation of animal rights and degradation of human rights were two sides of the same coin:

> Having equated animals with man, the Nazis proceeded to treat men as animals. By the time they were through, the first nation to ban vivisection had rendered countless innocent men, women, and children into lampshades and soap.[55]

They go on to show how present day animals rights activists, far from being embarrassed by Nazi associations, have no qualms about pressing the Holocaust into service for their own ends. According to Ingrid Newkirk, director of People for the Ethical Treatment of Animals (PeTA):

> Six million people died in concentration camps, but six billion broiler chickens will die this year in slaughterhouses.[56]

As Marquardt and her fellow authors observe:

> No Nazi could have said it better: the Holocaust was no worse than making chicken soup. The victims of Naziism got no worse than they gave to the chickens — they got their just deserts.[57]

The descent into the inferno of the gas ovens was partly the result of intellectual and philosophical confusion as to the meaning of 'rights':

> By assigning 'rights' to animals, which are by nature incapable of moral cognition, the Nazis annihilated the very concept of rights.[58]

In such a climate moral absolutes disappear and everything becomes relative. However, this confusion is undoubtedly more widespread today than it was in the 1930s. Many people would unhesitatingly assent to the notion that animals have rights, without considering the possible consequences of acting on that assumption.

The case against abortion is based on the moral imperative of the equal right to life of all human beings. But if humans are weighed against animals and found wanting, where does that leave such a right, especially for the majority of the population who do not object to killing animals? According to Ingrid Newkirk of PeTA:

> Animal liberationists do not separate out the human animal, so there is no rational basis for saying that a human being has special rights ... I don't believe that human beings have 'the right to life' ... This 'right to human life' I believe is another perversion.[59]

Although Green parties in different countries do not espouse exactly the same policies, they appear to be united in one important respect: their support for abortion. If human beings really are a form of pollution — a sort of cancer on the face of the earth — then it makes sense to cut the cancer out. Hence the attraction of the abortionist's knife to the Greens.

It is a paradox of environmentalism, particularly of the 'deep ecology' variety, that nature lovers whose hearts appear to bleed for the trees and the animals can be ruthless towards their own kind. For example, Dave Foreman of Earth First!, who proclaims his loyalty to 'the grizzly, the snail darter, the plankton ... to the rocks and streams'[60], once famously opposed food aid to the starving in Ethiopia:

> The worst thing we could do in Ethiopia is to give aid — the best thing would be to just let nature seek its own balance, to let the people there just starve.[61]

Going back to the earliest days of the modern environmental movement, Dixy Lee Ray quotes John Muir, who in 1892 founded The Sierra Club, one of the USA's most distinguished environmental groups, and who addressed alligators as follows:

> May you enjoy your lily pads and your aquatic grasses, secure in your undisturbed habitat. And may you occasionally enjoy a mouthful of terror-stricken man, by way of a dainty.[62]

This lack of compassion for fellow humans can only be explained by reference to the beliefs and values of those who hold such views. In an article for *Religion & Liberty*, the journal of the Acton Institute,

John Williams argued that inhuman cruelty is the inevitable outcome of glorifying or worshipping nature, because nature itself is cruel:

> Nature is not divine. It is the creation of God, not a god or a goddess. When treated as divine, the superficially benign face of nature is revealed for what it is. Invariably, human sacrifice is demanded. The worshippers of Ashtaroth and Baal did it. The Aztecs did it. The devotees of the eerie nature religion informing Nazism did it. Not surprisingly, the 'deep ecologists' recommend it.[63]

Throwing Spanners in the Works

The other key area in which Greens have succeeded in worsening the lot of human beings is in the field of overseas development projects.

Until recently it was accepted in development circles that human beings have equal rights to the highest possible material standard of living, whatever the colour of their skins and whichever part of the world they live in. This is now no longer the case. Jonathon Porritt has dismissed as 'meaningless' the 'vague inchoate liberal attachment to the notion that all people should share, at least to a degree, the sort of high standard of living which we ourselves enjoy'.[64]

Any major development project now will run into enormous opposition from Green organisations, complaining about the damage it will do to the environment. The first major success which they tasted in this field came in 1989 when they pressured the World Bank into suspending funding to a project to build a dam in Amazonia which would have provided hundreds of thousands of Brazilians with access to cheap hydro-electricity. The Greens objected that the dam would flood areas of rain forest, destroying wildlife and unsettling the forest Indians. The whole project was eventually scrapped.

The World Bank now has an Environmental Directorate to assess the environmental impact of every major project, and this procedure is followed by most national agencies. Those professionally involved in overseas aid projects make no secret of the fact that the well-being of human beings is no longer their unquestioned goal. According to the UK government's Overseas Development Administration:

> It is sometimes difficult to reconcile the objectives of conserving the environment in developing countries and alleviating poverty. The ODA's

policy is to ensure that measures to improve the environment should not have the effect of making poor people worse off.[65]

The wording of the last sentence is extremely significant. Until very recently its priorities would have been expressed in the reverse order.

The Greens like to chortle over the stifling influence they have had. Friends of the Earth boast that:

> Already we have helped to pressure the World Bank into reviewing its road building programmes and postponing a loan for a new dam in the Amazon.[66]

Even the reduction of mortality rates in the developing countries, which until recently would have been acclaimed by almost everyone as a good thing, is now challenged by those who advocate population control for the sake of the environment. In his book *Living Within Limits* American population guru Garrett Hardin demands that:

> ... birth control should precede death control ... continuing to give death control priority over birth control insures that populations will continue to increase ... Tender-mindedness, uninformed by carrying capacity thinking, may prevail in the short run, but in the long run such tender-mindedness will produce the tragedy of a population crash.[67]

Hardin quotes with approval the view of Alan Gregg, vice-president of the Rockefeller Foundation, that 'the world has cancer and ... the cancer cell is man', and that 'cancerous growths demand food; but ... they have never been cured by getting it'.[68]

The public expression of this point of view reached an all-time low in the British medical press with the publication in *The Lancet* of an article by Dr. Maurice King called *Health is a sustainable state*. In this he argued that some basic components of primary health care programmes, like oral rehydration of babies suffering from diarrhoea, should not be introduced into developing countries, on the basis that this would cause population growth by lowering the mortality rate.

He ended his article by calling for a redefinition of the role of the World Health Organisation, so that it will look after the health of the world and not just the people in it:

Such a strategy needs a name. Why not call it HSE 2100 — Health in a sustainable ecosystem for the year 2100? WHO has been exclusively concerned with the health of the *people* of the world. The recognition that their health is dependent on the health of the planet means that WHO now has a shared concern for the health of the planet as a whole. Only in this way will it ... truly become The *World* Health Organisation.[69]

When a distinguished medical periodical breaks out in such a nasty Green rash we need to monitor the progress of the infection.

Population and the Environment

I have argued so far that the demeaning view of man as a form of pollution which is put forward by Greens is incompatible with Christianity, because Christians believe that every human being is made in the image and likeness of God. To describe man as a pollutant is therefore a form of blasphemy.

However, there are many Christians who do not subscribe to this view of man as pollution, but who are still genuinely concerned that population growth is damaging the environment. After all, more people put out more rubbish. And if population growth has to be slowed down or reversed, how are Christians to square that with God's command to 'be fruitful, multiply, fill the earth and conquer it' (Gen.1:28)? Is it true that, as some Greens claim, the Bible was written for a less crowded world and cannot be taken literally now? We need to address the important question of whether or not population growth makes the environment better or worse.

The Political Ingredient

It is not the intention of any of the contributors to this volume to suggest that care of the environment is a trivial or undesirable pursuit. We all want to live in a good environment. No one wants to breathe polluted air or drink poisoned water or eat rotten food. Men and women have always striven to make their surroundings as comfortable, convenient and attractive as possible. The Greens did not invent 'the environment' or the idea that it should be cared for.

It has to be admitted that the idea that population growth will make the environment worse has a certain logical appeal. More people will consume more resources; they will require more houses; more power supplies; more cars. How will the planet cope?

Environmental problems, like most of the problems which are blamed on population growth, are certainly real enough problems, but they are being attributed to the wrong causes. Like poverty, famine and unemployment (which have all been blamed on 'the population explosion') they are basically political and economic in origin.

To solve environmental problems you need two things: the political will to tackle the problem and the level of resources to pay for the solution. Countries which are rich and free will therefore always have better environments than countries which are poor and oppressed.

We received striking proof of this with the collapse of the Iron Curtain and the opening up of Eastern Europe. Under communism whole towns and communities were poisoned by toxic waste, huge amounts of radioactive waste were discharged into inland waterways, and the Aral Sea itself dried up to a poisonous little lake by foolish industrial policies.[70] The poverty and permanent shortage of resources which characterised communist economies meant that the means were never available to take the necessary steps to reduce pollution, and under a tyrannical system which made freedom of association impossible, it was clearly out of the question for the people to protest.

Clearly the pollution of Eastern Europe had nothing to do with population growth. Most Eastern European countries had a lower population density and lower birthrates than were common in the West. Indeed, East Germany and Hungary were amongst the first countries in the world to start losing population in absolute numbers.

We should remember that in communist countries industry is supposedly run for the benefit of the proletariat, whereas in the West it is run to generate profits for shareholders. In spite of this, industrial activity in the West is both *more* intense and *less* polluting, because we regulate industrial processes to ensure minimum despoliation of the environment. As Michael Howard said when he was Minister for Water, the reason that most British sewage is treated, whereas in Bangladesh most sewage is untreated, is that Britain is a rich country and Bangladesh is a poor one.

An important addition has been made to our understanding of the relationship between politics and the environment by American economist Mikhail Bernstam. In his monograph *The Wealth of Nations and the Environment*[71] he argues that the issues of pollution and resource consumption are directly linked to the political and economic structures of countries. Illustrating his argument with statistics from official sources, he shows that the innate tendency of socialist or planned economies is to consume more resources, create less output and produce more pollution. The tendency of capitalist or market economies is to consume fewer resources to create more output and generate less pollution.

Here are some of Bernstam's findings, based on a comparison of the capitalist USA and the communist USSR:

* Pollutant emissions from the average motor vehicle in the USSR in the late 1980s were nine times higher than in the USA. The gap would be greater if planes were included.

* For every $1,000 of Gross National Product (GNP) the USSR produced between 2.5 times and 5.8 times as much pollution from transport and stationary sources (e.g. power stations).

* In the USA energy consumption per $1,000 of GNP declined at 1 per cent per year between 1929-89.

* Resource consumption per unit of GNP is about three times higher in socialist countries than it is in market economies. In the second half of the 1980s the Soviet Union consumed over one and a half times as much steel as the USA to produce about three quarters of the volume of metal originated machinery and other producer goods.

Bernstam found that during the 1970s and 1980s there were *falls* in the per capita energy consumption of the market economies of Europe and the USA, while per capita consumption was steadily rising in the USSR. Throughout the period living standards were higher in the West and rising, especially in terms of all the consumer goods we take for granted which use energy like cars, videos and computers, while the standard of living in the USSR was much lower and falling. We were able to make less energy do much, much more.

Bernstam shows that the trends in the West cannot be attributed to the rise of the Green movement and the rash of environmental legislation which characterised the 1970s and especially the 1980s: they go back much further. He also manages to counter the familiar Green argument that we must accept economic stagnation because further growth would mean more pollution. Bernstam argues that, on the contrary, as economic growth is impossible without technological progress, and as that technological progress 'cannot but eventually reduce resource use and environmental discharges', then 'long-term economic growth is impossible without environmental improvements'.[72]

Bernstam warns that 'the future of world environmental conditions depends to a significant extent on the choice of economic system in developing countries'.[73] Put simply, this means that the spread of market economies will lead to a better global environment, and the spread of socialist or centrally planned economies will make it worse. This is a prescription which most Greens would find revolting, given their deep-seated hostility towards markets.

Good News from Africa

Africa is a continent which is frequently held up by the population control/environmental lobby as an example of the horrors of population growth. More people are equated with more poverty and a more degraded environment. It is therefore doubly significant that the most important work which has recently emerged to squash these assumptions has come from Africa.

In their book *More People, Less Erosion* Mary Tiffen, Michael Mortimore and Francis Gichuki give a detailed picture of the Machakos District of Kenya between 1930-89. The area has been intensively studied and written about over the period, giving good records of changes in soil management, crops, livestock, rainfall, social institutions and every other variable which might affect development.

During the period under review the population of the area increased by more than five times but, far from causing famine as Malthusian theory would predict, agricultural output went up by three times per head of population, and by *more than ten times per acre*. Machakos had, in fact, proved to be the perfect illustration of the theory first put forward by Ester Boserup in 1965 that population growth is a vital pre-condition of agricultural development, and of economic progress in general. This is because the increased demand for food forces farmers to adopt more intensive methods which would not be worthwhile at lower population densities, like moving from forest fallow to ploughing with oxen. Increasing population densities make the creation of infrastructure like roads possible; and as technological advances enable fewer farmers to produce more food, other sectors of the workforce are released to engage in different types of productive activity. For these and other reasons Boserup came to the conclusion that 'population increase is a condition for economic development in its first stages'[74] and that 'primitive communities with sustained population growth have a better chance to get into a process of genuine economic development than primitive communities with stagnant or declining population'.[75]

The authors of *More People, Less Erosion* found incontrovertible evidence that Ester Boserup had been right. Population growth had actually propelled the people of Machakos into economic development, and there was nothing to suggest that the Machakos experience was unique:

> ... it appears to be beyond doubt that low levels of population density are inimical to technology change. Access to markets and knowledge depends on social and physical infrastructure, especially roads, schools, and extension. The per capita cost of provision remains high until there has been quite a marked increase in density.[76]

However the most significant aspect of their findings was that this great advance in terms of production had not been achieved at the expense of the environment, as Green doomsayers are constantly telling us must be the case. On the contrary, the increase in production coupled with population growth had led to considerable improvements in the environment.

Environmental problems such as soil erosion, which had led some colonial observers to describe parts of Machakos as irreversibly degraded in the 1930s, and already populated far beyond the carrying capacity of the land, had been dealt with. Furthermore, they had been dealt with *because of* the population growth. The loss of soil owing to heavy rains following upon long periods of sparse rainfall was stopped by the construction of bench terraces on the hillsides. These retained moisture as well as stopping the soil erosion. Terracing is a labour-intensive technology: it requires many available pairs of hands, coupled with a sufficient demand for the food which can be produced to make it worth the farmers' while.

The book is illustrated by a remarkable series of 'before' and 'after' photographs, showing landscapes which were described as 'irreversibly degraded' in the 1930s now producing crops and covered with trees.

More People, Less Erosion ends with a warning to those who promote population control programmes based upon the supposed 'needs' of the environment:

> The provision of family planning information and the making accessible of supplies can be justified as adding to peoples' choices and the control which they have over their circumstances. To argue for population limitation on environmental grounds weakens the case for it both theoretically and practically.[77]

In his book *The Myth of Overpopulation* Patrick Darling has compiled an overview of the research to emerge from Africa in recent years which shows how population growth has sometimes accompanied *improvements* to the environment, and how the one is indeed often dependent upon the other.[78] For example:

> ... in the Kano close-settled zone of Northern Nigeria ... studies show increasing population densities over the centuries going hand-in-hand with *increasing* tree densities, small livestock numbers and crop yields, without any discernible loss in soil fertility ... Population pressure causing the deforestation of Kano proves to be just another discredited, dry-season, 'rural tourist' myth ...[79]

Darling also remarks that:

> A nationwide survey of smallholder farmers in Kenya shows that, as densities increase, the percentage of farmers planting trees goes up, livestock ownership rises, more milk is sold and more manure and other inputs are used; and these characteristics hold true under different agro-ecological conditions.[80]

There is no reason to believe that population growth will make the environment worse, or that population shrinkage will make it better. We can have more people *and* less pollution, as long as we are prepared to pay for environmental improvements, and as long as we continue to use the intelligence which God has given us to develop new

83

technologies which will continue to improve the quality of life on earth. It is not necessary for friends of the earth to be enemies of the people.

Sour Greens

This analysis will not convince the Greens for two reasons. Firstly, because they maintain that science and technology are the source of problems, not their solution. It is not unusual to hear leading spokespersons describe every step in the progress of the human race as a calamity for the planet, from the discovery of coal to the discovery of penicillin.[81] According to Jonathon Porritt:

> ... every advance that technology has brought us ... has brought with it social and ecological problems — which more than outweigh the benefits that have been derived from its development.[82]

The Greens believe that the game is very nearly up, and that all of our life-support systems which have been achieved at the expense of the planet are about to collapse:

> Humanity stands at the edge of an abyss. Unless we make the right choices ... we shall go over that edge — irrevocably.[83]

Secondly, the very fact that technological progress enables more people to enjoy a higher standard of living is a *minus not a plus* to the Greens as they don't want to see humans occupying any more of the planet to start with. In his book *The Greening of the Church* Fr. Sean McDonagh argues that the regulation of population is necessary 'to meet the demands of social justice and *the rights of other species'* (emphasis added),[84] while American ecologist Garrett Hardin regards the fall in infant mortality in Africa as 'disastrous'.[85] Paul and Anne Ehrlich described the agricultural revolution (once referred to as the green revolution) which increased food production to an unprecedented degree by the application of technology, and made the complete elimination of famine a possibility for the first time in history, as perhaps 'the greatest mistake that ever occurred in the biosphere — a mistake not just for homo sapiens but for the integrity of all ecosystems'.[86] Most revealing of all, however, was the reaction of environmentalists to the news that scientists had perfected the technique of cold fusion, which would have given us limitless supplies of cheap energy. In fact the announcement was premature because the experiment could not be replicated but, had the claims been true, everyone in the world could have easily enjoyed a Western, energy-intensive lifestyle. Paul Ehrlich described the possibility of universal cheap energy as 'like giving a machine gun to an idiot child'[87] while Jeremy Rifkin told *The Los Angeles Times* that 'it's the worst thing that could happen to our planet'.[88]

Triumph to Tragedy

One of the most effective attacks on the junk science which lies at the heart of the Green movement was written by American scientist Dixy Lee Ray and journalist Lou Guzzo. Their book *Trashing the Planet* [89] exploded many of the myths surrounding such issues as global warming, nuclear waste, acid rain and asbestos. Perhaps its saddest chapter was the one which dealt with the banning of DDT, and it is worth summarising the argument here as it tells us so much about the feelings of the Greens for their fellow human beings, and the consequences of the high-profile Green campaigns in the real world.

Ray and Guzzo describe DDT as a tale of triumph that ended in tragedy. It was patented as an insecticide in 1939 and proved its worth during the Second World War when it was used by the Allied troops to control typhus. It was so effective that no Allied soldier was stricken by typhus for the first time in the history of warfare. (During World War I more soldiers died from typhus than from bullets.)

However DDT really came into its own as a measure to combat the malaria-carrying mosquito. It was so spectacularly successful that malaria cases in Sri Lanka fell from 2.8 million in 1948, before spraying started, to 17 (seventeen) in 1963. In 1969 the US Agency for International Development reported that malaria *deaths* in India had fallen from 750,000 per year to 1,500 per year.[90] By 1970, 79 percent of all people living in malarial regions were protected and it was expected that malaria would soon be completely eradicated. Then the Greens got on to DDT.

1962 saw the publication of Rachel Carson's book *Silent Spring*,[91] the mother of all Green scaremongering books. Described by Stephen Fox, the historian of the conservation movement, as 'the *Uncle Tom's*

Cabin of modern environmentalism,'[92] in many ways it marked the emergence of the militant, campaigning Green lobby. It accused modern man of poisoning the environment with chemicals, and DDT was singled out for special attack. Others took up the standard, and the charges against DDT began to mount. It was supposed to be causing cancer, building up in the food chain and poisoning the landscape and the waterways. It was also said to be causing the decline of certain bird populations, including birds of prey.

However, DDT is not carcinogenic in humans, and no one was in any danger of being poisoned by it. The traces which were turning up in the environment were so tiny — one part *per trillion* in inshore waters — that they could never have harmed anyone. A group of volunteers were dosed with comparatively huge amounts over more than two years. They suffered no ill effects then or in the nearly 30 years since. The World Health Organisation studied groups of people who had been exposed to large doses of DDT, sometimes by having the interiors of their houses sprayed regularly for over 20 years, and reported that 'the only confirmed cases of injury have been the result of massive accidental or suicidal ingestion'.[93] Furthermore DDT is not persistent in the environment; 93 percent of all DDT is broken down in sea water in 38 days.

The charges concerning the effect on bird populations have been more difficult to resolve. DDT was said to be poisoning some species, particularly birds of prey, and leading to reproductive failure by causing a thinning of eggshells. In spite of this, populations of ospreys had been increasing throughout the period of DDT use, and although peregrine falcons were declining, they had been declining since the 1890s. Attempts to replicate egg-thinning were made by dosing birds with large amounts of DDT, but no conclusive evidence was found.[94]

The various charges against DDT resulted in a public hearing in the USA, which eventually decided there was no need for a ban. Two months later, on 14 June 1972, William Ruckelshaus, Administrator of the Environmental Protection Agency, banned all uses of it. This was effectively a world wide ban as it meant that no nation receiving US aid could ever use it.

Why did Ruckelshaus do it, against so much scientific evidence and ignoring the World Health Organisation's warning that 'for the present, no economic alternative to DDT is available and the epidemiological, operational and financial consequences of the withdrawal of DDT would be very grave'?[95] Years later he admitted that 'decisions by the government involving the use of toxic substances are political ... [and] the ultimate judgement remains political'.[96]

But what sort of politics could lie behind a decision which resulted in millions of preventable deaths? Because, with DDT out of the way, malaria came back. Six years after the US ban of DDT there were 800 million cases of malaria and 8.2 million deaths per year.

Ray and Guzzo suggest that the eagerness to ban DDT was related to its very success. During the less than 30 years of its use (1944-72) it prevented more human deaths than any other man-made chemical in history. It also opened up land which had previously been unsuitable for human habitation. This was not welcome news to those concerned with world population growth. Dr Charles Wursta, who was then chief scientist for the Environmental Defence Fund, told a journalist who asked him about banning DDT that in his opinion there were too many people in the world and 'this is as good a way to get rid of them as any',[97] while Alexander King, a British scientist working for the government who had been involved with the introduction of DDT for use in the forces during the Second World War, later complained of its civilian use:

> In Guyana, within two years its had almost eliminated malaria but at the same time the birthrate had doubled. So my chief quarrel with DDT in hindsight is that it has added greatly to the population problem.[98]

Ray and Guzzo estimate that there are now between 60 and 100 million deaths annually as a result of the banning or restriction of the chemicals which could have prevented them.[99] This is the real cost of Greenery. Needless to say, it will not be met by the white, middle class Westerners who run the movement.

What is a Good Environment?

I began this chapter by saying that the absorption of the population control movement by the Green lobby gave a new lease of life to arguments that populations should be reduced, because instead of having to justify the policies in the name of human well-being, it was only necessary now to speak of the 'needs' of the planet.

Such a concept is, however, antithetical to Christian cosmology which makes it quite clear, throughout the Old and the New Testament, that the natural order, the 'biosphere', the planet or whatever you want to call it, can have no 'rights' against man, who is made in God's image, and no 'needs' which can be met at man's expense.

Problems can arise for Christians and Greens, when discussing the question of whether or not population growth can be reconciled with a good environment, because there is not necessarily a shared view of what constitutes a good environment. Does it mean a setting in which men and women can exercise their talents and pursue their aspirations to their maximum benefit? Or does it mean a wild and uncultivated landscape in which the hand of man has never been seen? It is because some Greens would have us believe that they prefer the latter that discussion becomes difficult.

At a deeper level, what do we mean by environment? An environment is something which environs or surrounds, but what does it surround? The traditional view would have been that it surrounds man. To the Greens, however, the environment (by which they mean the natural world) has an integrity of its own. Rats, locusts, the tsetse fly, moss and even 'the wilderness' are all life forms meriting respect. Man is nothing special. They have even added another 'ism' to the vocabulary of political correctness: the assumption that man's needs should take precedence over those of other life-forms is condemned as 'speciesism'.

In his book *The Greening of the Church* Fr. Sean McDonagh praises the attitudes towards nature of the American Indians and the aborigines for whom:

> Nature has its own meaning and purpose irrespective of its value to humans. Christianity … [has] much to learn from this approach to the natural world.[100]

Man's Ultimate Environment

However, for the Christian, there is an even more profound aspect to this debate. As Arthur Kay has argued in *Calvinism Today*,[101] man's ultimate environment is God: 'In Him we live and move and have our being' (Acts 17:28). This point of view is explored by Paul Haffner in the last chapter of this volume.

For this reason, Christians take a particular view of the problems experienced in this life. They are not the most important thing to us, because they pale into insignificance compared with the eternal destiny of every man and woman who has been created by God in His own image.

It is exactly because of the Christian concern with the next life that Greens become so impatient with Christians. For the Greens, including some who would regard themselves as Christians, or at least as religious, it is *this life* which is important. Jonathon Porritt describes himself as:

> ... unorthodox in my Christianity and ... part of my unorthodoxy is that I am not concerned about what happens to my soul after death. But I do care, passionately, about what happens to me and to you and indeed to the totality of life on Earth while I am here ... I think that the Churches' preoccupation of life after death has been at the expense of a concern for life before death.[102]

The Dilemma for Christians

As we have already said, care for the environment is both legitimate and praiseworthy. Many Christians feel called to participate in what they regard as a ministry for our times. The dilemma for environmentally aware Christians begins when they take up the baggage of Greenery, including those parts which we have argued above are in conflict with the values of their Judaeo-Christian inheritance.

Christians who campaign for population control find little support in scripture. God's instruction to Adam and Eve to be fruitful and multiply (Gen. 1:28) was repeated in his covenants with Noah (Gen. 9:7) and with Abraham (Gen. 17:6). Fertility and large families are constantly associated with God's blessing (Ps. 113:9; Ps. 127:3-5; Gen. 22:17; 2 Kings 4:12-17; Deut. 7:14), whilst sterility is a misfortune or even a sign of God's disfavour (Hos.9:11-14; 2 Sam.6:23; Gen.16:2). As Calvin Beisner puts it:

> The Bible ... sees population growth as a blessing, not a curse. Not the *explosion* of population but the *blossoming* of population. We are not the population bomb but the population bloom. People aren't pollution, we're the solution.[103]

Arguments for population control which attempt to enlist Biblical authority are unconvincing. For example, the American theologian Edward Echlin attaches great significance for the modern world and its 'eco-population crisis' to the fact that Jesus was 'unmarried, unattached and *almost certainly childless*' (emphasis added). He claims that although Jesus 'never, as far as we know, addressed the problem of over-population', he nevertheless set us a 'gleaming example':

> His relationships were cosmic, men and women friends together caring for all people, for the earth, and for the future without necessarily having 'their own' children.[104]

Many Christians would be made uneasy by this interpretation of the marital and parental status of Jesus. It recalls the Christmas card produced by the Planned Parenthood Federation of America which depicted the Holy Family with the message 'God had only one Son: Follow HIS example — Visit your local Planned Parenthood'.

The Swamp Thing

Because Christians believe in the unique nature of every human being, made in the image and likeness of God, it becomes impossible to subscribe to the notion that human beings can ever be a form of pollution. Nor can Christians easily envisage an earth which has been 'spoiled' by too many people who are crowding out the animals. As Arthur Kay has shown, 'the Bible repeatedly indicates that man's government (even that of the Canaanites) is to be preferred over that of wild beasts (Exod. 23:28-29, Job 30:29, Isa. 13:21, 34:11-15, Jer. 50:39)'.[105]

Perhaps nothing indicates the different perspectives which Greens and Christians can have on the environment more succinctly than the growing feelings that 'wilderness' and 'wetlands' have their own integrity, and should be protected from human interference.

Draining swamps has traditionally been regarded as one of the great achievements of human civilisations. The building of Rome was made possible by the draining of the Pontine marshes; much of present day Holland was reclaimed from the sea in the 17th century by means of dams and dikes; and the 'Backs' at Cambridge — one of the most beautiful landscapes in Europe — was created by draining the marshes in the 18th and 19th centuries. The Capitol and the White House in Washington stand on former swamps. It is almost certain that any attempt to carry out such works now would meet with intense opposition from environmental lobbyists. An article in *People and the Planet*, the journal of the International Planned Parenthood Federation, complains about fishermen who have been guilty of 'degrading coastal resources by converting large areas of wetlands and mangrove swamps into fish and shellfish ponds'.[106] It would appear that to convert swamps for human benefit is now a 'degrading' step.

In 1915 a Congregational hymn put what was then a fairly standard view of wilderness:

> The wilderness is planted,
> The deserts bloom and sing;
> On coast and plain the cities
> Their smokey banners fling.

This positive view of 'smokey banners' as the triumphant proclamation of wilderness tamed puts the world-view of this hymn-writer a long way from our own. As Alexander Volokh wrote in *Reason*, 'This was back when it was unheard of to oppose a policy with the question, "Ah, but how will it affect the trout?"'.[107]

This response to policy is now far from unheard-of, but to protect 'wilderness' and swamps the light green arguments about 'sustainable development' will not suffice. We are now into dark green territory, in which wilderness assumes a spiritual significance. A fundraising letter sent out by The Wilderness Society in the USA claimed that wilderness areas need to be protected because:'destroy them and we destroy our spirit ... destroy them and we destroy our sense of values'.[108] This is pretty heavy theological stuff, far removed from any known branch of science. Under this scenario, humans are a form of pollution the earth could do without. In his book *How to Think about the Earth* philosopher Stephen Clark quotes Simone Weil who wrote:

> When I am anywhere, I pollute the silence of earth and sky with my breathing and the beating of my heart.[109]

and the Green poet R. Jeffers:

Whatever we do to a landscape — even to look — damages it.[110]

Clark's comment is:

Our aim should be to glimpse the world as it would be, as it is, without our gaze.[111]

The Bible does not share this romantic view of wilderness. As P. J. O'Rourke points out:

In the Old Testament, six Hebrew words are translated as *wilderness*. The literal meanings of the words are 'a desolation', 'a worthless thing', 'a sterile valley', 'an arid region', 'a haunt of wild beasts and nomads' and 'an open field'. In the New Testament the two Greek words for *wilderness* both mean 'lonely place'.[112]

The Genesis account of creation makes it very clear that Adam and Eve represented the crowning glory of the process. After every other stage God 'saw that it was good' but after creating man he saw that 'it was very good' (Gen. 1:31). Isaiah tells us that when God created the world he meant it to be 'no chaos, but a place to be lived in' (Is. 45:18), while King Uzziah, who 'did what is pleasing to Yahweh ... built towers in the wilderness ... and dug a great many cisterns, for ... he was fond of agriculture' (2 Chron. 26:4,10-11).

This biblical perspective contrasts strongly with the view of some leading Greens that the practice of agriculture itself was a sort of 'original sin' of the environmental 'fall', when man ceased to live the life of scavenger and began to take control of the natural order. Dave Foreman, founder of the radical environmental group Earth First!, puts the case as follows:

Before agriculture was midwifed in the Middle East, humans were in the wilderness. We had no concept of 'wilderness' because everything was wilderness and we were part of it. But with irrigation ditches, crop surpluses, and permanent villages, we became apart from the natural world and substituted our fields, habitations, temples and storehouses. Between the wilderness that created us and the civilization created by us, grew an ever-widening rift.[113]

This environmental account of the 'fall', when man in his pride began to control nature instead of humbly accepting whatever her bounty bestowed, is a common theme of Green writers. In a celebrated and much-quoted passage from a book review in *The Los Angeles Times* David Graber, a biologist working for the National Parks Service, offered this jeremiad:

> I know social scientists who remind me that people are part of nature, but it isn't true. Somewhere along the line — about a billion years ago, maybe half that — we quit the contract and became a cancer. We have become a plague upon ourselves and upon the Earth ... Until such time as Homo sapiens should decide to rejoin Nature, some of us can only hope for the right virus to come along.[114]

The ability to control our environment, rather than be controlled by it, is one of the distinguishing features of homo sapiens. Whereas an animal is totally dependent for survival on the presence of environmental factors such as warmth, moisture, grass and so on, we can make ourselves comfortable anywhere by using our rational skills. Men have walked on the surface of the moon, whereas rain forest insects are said to be unable to survive beyond their own part of the forest. It is precisely this adaptability which seems to disturb the Greens. According to Norman Myers:

> Wherever we look, we see our own image reflected back in some form or other — the apotheosis of hubris-ridden humanity ... We have sought to elevate ourselves above the natural world, and too often we do it with the selective discretion of Neanderthals.[115]

Some Greens hate their own species for its unique abilities, and it is this hatred which lies behind the bloodchilling anathemas which pour from their lips. According to Dave Foreman of Earth First!:

> I see no solution to our ruination of Earth except for a drastic reduction of the human population[116] ... It may well take our extinction to set things straight.[117]

We can only hope that the Greens will never be in a position to carry out their vision. As Virginia Postrel said in the conclusion to her article in *Reason*, they only need 'an opportunity and a Lenin'.[118]

The Christian Approach

It is right that Christians should concern themselves with environmental problems. Making the physical world a better place to live in is one of the ways in which we can be the salt of the earth. However Christians are now being called upon to exercise a special ministry to the environmental movement, and that is to inject into it the values and priorities of the Bible. We need to state, clearly and unequivocally, that the environment was made for man, not man for the environment.

NOTES

1. Club of Rome, Alexander King and Bertrand Schneider, *The First Global Revolution*, New York: Pantheon Books, (1991) p. 115, Quoted in Dixy Lee Ray with Lou Guzzo, *Environmental Overkill: Whatever Happened to Common Sense?*, Washington: Regnery Gateway (1993) p. 205.

2. Rachel Carson, *Silent Spring*, Boston: Houghton Mifflin Co. (1962).

3. Donella H. Meadows, Dennis L. Meadows, Jorgen Randers and William W. Behrens III, *The Limits to Growth*, London: Earth Island (1972) pp. 54 ff.

4. Robert Stavins, 'Comments on Lethal Model 2: "The Limits to Growth Revisited" by William Nordhaus', in *Brookings Papers on Economic Activity* (1993) quoted by Lynn Scarlett, 'Clear Thinking About the Earth' in John A. Baden, *Environmental Gore: A Constructive Response to Earth in the Balance*, San Francisco: Pacific Research Institute (1994) p. 252.

5. Fred Pearce, *Turning Up The Heat: Our Perilous Future in the Global Greenhouse*, London: Bodley Head (1989) p. 177.

6. Speech by Barber Conable, President of the World Bank, to IPPF Members' Assembly in Ottawa (November 1989) reprinted in *People* Vol.17 No. 2, London: International Planned Parenthood Federation (1990) pp. 3-5

7. Jonathon Porritt, 'Stewards of the Earth', *The Ampleforth Journal*

(Spring 1991) p. 43.

8. Norman Myers (ed.), *The Gaia Atlas of Planet Management*, London: Pan Books (1985) pp. 19, 18.

9. Frank Barnaby (ed.), *The Gaia Peace Atlas*, London: Pan Books (1988) p. 111.

10. Norman Myers (ed.), *The Gaia Atlas of Planet Management*, London: Pan Books (1985) p. 20

11. Sean McDonagh, *The Greening of the Church*, London: Geoffrey Chapman (1990) p. 65.

12. Thomas Berry, 'The Dream of the Future: Our Way into the Future', *Cross Currents*, Summer/Fall 1987, p. 210, quoted in Paul Collins, *God's Earth: Religion as if Matter Really Mattered*, Dublin: Gill and MacMillan, 1995, p. 21

13. Quoted from Stephen Hawking's Channel 4 TV series *Reality on the Rocks* in Robert Crampton, 'Intelligence Test', *The Times* magazine, 8 April 1995.

14. Paul Watson's view that 'We, the human species, have become a viral epidemic to the Earth, in truth, the AIDS of the Earth' is quoted in Troy Mader, 'The Enemy Within', *Abundant Wildlife* (September 1992) p. 4.

15. Greenpeace leaflet *Thank God Someone's Making Waves* (undated).

16. James T. Boulton and Andrew Robertson (eds.), *The Letters of D.H. Lawrence, Vol.III, 1916-21*, Cambridge University Press, (1984) p. 160; Quoted in John Carey, *The Intellectuals and the Masses: Pride and Prejudice Among The Literary Intelligentsia 1880 - 1939*, Faber and Faber (1992) pp. 11-12.

17. James T. Boulton (ed.), *The Letters of D.H. Lawrence, Vol.I, 1901-13*, Cambridge University Press (1979) p. 81; Quoted in John Carey, op.cit. p. 12.

18. George Bernard Shaw, Preface to *On The Rocks* in *Complete Prefaces*, London: Paul Hamlyn (1965); quoted in John Carey. op.cit.. p. 63.

19. See David Bodanis, *Web of Words: The Ideas Behind Politics*, London: Macmillan Press (1988) pp. 15-38; and quoted in John Carey,. op.cit.. p. 26.

20. John Carey, op.cit.. p. 206.

21. The first two quotations are from John Fowles, author of *The French Lieutenant's Woman*, who continues 'I cannot imagine that we rampant, myopic and insatiably self-centred creatures should be allowed to survive a single day more'; the third is from popular zoologist

Desmond Morris. See Jonathon Porritt, *Save the Earth*, Dorling Kindersley (21991) pp. 45 and 115.

22. For an account of the impact of Chinese population policies on ordinary women and men see Steven W. Mosher, *A Mother's Ordeal: One Woman's Fight Against China's One-Child Policy*, London: Little, Brown and Company (1994).

23. For a fuller account of the ways in which population control programmes violate freedom and choice and the reproductive rights of women see Robert Whelan, *Choices in Childbearing: When Does Family Planning Become Population Control?*, London: Committee on Population and the Economy (1992).

24. *Sunday Times* magazine (26 February 1989).

25. Editorial 'Dinosaurs and Destiny', *The Economist* (28 December 1988). Quoted in Dixy Lee Ray and Lou Guzzo, *Trashing the Planet*, New York: Harper Collins (1992) p. 169

26. Tom Regan (ed.), *Earthbound: New Introductory Readings in Environmental Ethics*, New York: Random House (1984) p. 269. Quoted in John K. Williams, 'Gary Cooper, Humane Existence and Deep Ecology', *Religion & Liberty*, Grand Rapids, MI: The Acton Institute (Autumn 1992).

27. According to the *Earth First!* newsletter, cited in *Access to Energy*, Vol.17, No.4 (December 1989): 'If radical environmentalists were to invent a disease to bring human populations back to sanity it would probably be something like AIDS. It has the potential to end industrialism, which is the main force behind the environmental crises'. See also Miss Ann Thropy (pseudonym) 'Population and AIDS', *Earth First!* (1 May 1987) p. 32 and Daniel Conner, 'Is AIDS the Answer to an Environmentalist's Prayer?', *Earth First!* (22 December 1987) pp. 14-16.

28. 'Eco-Kamikazes Wanted', *Earth First!* (22 September 1989) p. 21.

29. 'Les U. Knight' (pseudonym), 'Voluntary Human Extinction', *Wild Earth*, Vol.1 No. 2 (Summer 1991) p. 72.

30. Foreword by HRH Prince Philip to Fleur Cowles, *People as Animals*, London: Robin Clark (1986).

31. *Policy Pointers: Population*, The Green Party (March 1989).

32. Sara Parkin, *Green Parties: An International Guide: Policies for a Green Future* London: Heretic Books (1989) p. 334.

33. Sandy Irvine and Alec Ponton, *A Green Manifesto*, London: Macdonald Optima (1988) p. 23.

34. Ibid.
35. Ibid.
36. Comment made on *Clive James Late Show*, BBC2 (3 March 1989).
37. 'New Architect for art's grand design', *The Sunday Express* (11 September 1988).
38. Jeffrey McNeely, 'Diverse nature, diverse cultures', *People and the Planet*, Vol. 2 No. 3, London: International Planned Parenthood Federation (1993) p. 12.
39. Edward Goldsmith, *The Way: An Ecological World View*, London: Rider (1992) p. 288.
40. Frank Barnaby (ed.) *The Gaia Peace Atlas*, Pan Books (1988) p. 160 and 170.
41. Quoted in *Earthwatch*, No 41 (1991) p.18. *Earthwatch* was an environmental supplement to *People*, the magazine of the International Planned Parenthood Federation.
42. 'Beauty and the Beasts', *The Sunday Telegraph* (19 December 1993).
43. Interviewed by Tatler, 'Out to Lunch', *The Sunday Express* magazine (16 December 1990).
44. Quoted in David Moller, 'Terrorists Who Wage War on Medicine', *The Reader's Digest* (July 1991).
45. Interview from *The man who named the world*, Channel 4 (1 July 1990).
46. James Lovelock, 'Green science: an alliance for the coming world war', *The Sunday Times* (1 October 1989).
47. HRH The Duke of Edinburgh, 'The Future Countryside', *RSA Journal*, London: Royal Society of Arts (August 1988).
48. Randy T. Simmons and Urs P. Kreuter, 'Banning Ivory Sales: No Way to Save the Elephant', *Policy*, Vol.6, No.3, St. Leonard's, Australia (1990) pp. 26-29; Fred Bridgland,'Rebel Africans to defy ivory ban', *The Sunday Telegraph* (16 July 1989); Ike Sugg and Urs Kreuter, *Elephants and Ivory: Lessons from the Trade Ban*, London: Institute of Economic Affairs (1994).
49. Undated letter to 'Violet Fane', written between 1887-89, reprinted in Merlin Holland (ed.), *Oscar Wilde: Letters and Essays*, London: The Folio Society, (1993) p. 32.
50. Jim Mason and Peter Singer, *Animal Factories*, New York: Crown Publishers (1980), quoted in Kathleen Marquardt *et al*. *Animal Scam: The Beastly Abuse of Human Rights*, Washington: Regnery Gateway (1993) p. 129
51. Martin Morse Wooster, 'Monuments to Slain Trees', *Reason* (April

1990) pp. 41-2.

52. Nazi propaganda magazine cited in Christopher Paul Roberts, 'National Socialism and the Modern Animal Rights Movement: Some Interesting Parallels', Northeastern University (1990). Quoted in David R. Zimmerman, 'Activists Use Anti-Semitic Tactics', *Probe* (1 June 1992) p. 6.

53. F. Kersten, *The Kersten Memoirs 1940-5*, tr. C. Fitzgibbons and J. Oliver, Macmillan (1956) p. 115f.

54. Hermann Göring, 'A Broadcast Over the German Radio Network Describing the Fight Against Vivisection and the Measures Taken to Prohibit It' (August 28 1933) in *The Political Testament of Hermann Göring*, trans. H. W. Blood-Ryan, London: John Long (1939) p.73. Quoted in Kathleen Marquardt *et al.* op. cit., p. 124

55. Kathleen Marquardt *et al.* op. cit., p. 125.

56. Quoted in Chip Brown, 'She's a Portrait of Zealotry in Plastic Shoes', *Washington Post* (13 November 1983) p. B10.

57. Kathleen Marquardt *et al.*, op. cit., p.126.

58. Ibid., p. 125.

59. Quoted in Katie McCabe, 'Who Will Live, Who Will Die?' *Washingtonian*, 21, No 11 (August 1986) p. 115; and in Charles Griswold Jr., 'Q & A', *Washington City Paper* (20 December 1985) p. 44.

60. 'Earth First Surfaces in Forest', *Spokane Chronicle* (4 July 1988). Quoted in Michael Coffman, op.cit, p. 93.

61. Dave Foreman, letter to the editor, *The Nation* (12 December 1987). Quoted in Michael Coffman, op.cit., p. 93.

62. Quoted in Dixy Lee Ray with Lou Guzzo, *Environmental Overkill*, op.cit., p. 204.

63. John K. Williams, 'Gary Cooper, Humane Existence and Deep Ecology', *Religion & Liberty*, Grand Rapids, MI: The Acton Institute (Autumn 1992) p. 15.

64. Jonathon Porritt, 'Stewards of the Earth', op.cit., p. 45.

65. Overseas Development Administration, Briefing Paper 3, *Sustainable Development* (undated).

66. Friends of the Earth leaflet 'Tropical Rain Forest', (circa November 1988).

67. Garrett Hardin, *Living Within Limits: Ecology, Economics and Population Taboos*, Oxford: Oxford University Press (1993) p. 177.

68. Alan Gregg, 'A Medical Aspect of the Population Problem', *Science*,

Vol 121 (1955) pp.681-2. Quoted in Garett Hardin, op.cit., pp. 174-5.

69. Maurice King, 'Health is a sustainable state', *The Lancet*, Vol. 336 (September 15 1990) pp. 664-667.

70. See Mike Edwards, 'Lethal Legacy: Pollution in the former USSR', *National Geographic* (August 1994).

71. Mikhail S. Bernstam, *The Wealth of Nations and the Environment*, London: Institute of Economic Affairs (1991).

72. Mikhail S. Bernstam., op. cit., p. 41.

73. Ibid., p. 59.

74. Ester Boserup, *The Conditions of Agricultural Growth: The Economics of Agrarian Change under Population Pressure*, London: Earthscan Publications (1993) p. 74.

75. Ibid., p. 118.

76. Mary Tiffen, Michael Mortimore and Francis Gichuki, *More People, Less Erosion: Environmental Recovery in Kenya*, Chichester: John Wiley and Sons (1994) p. 271.

77. Ibid., p. 284.

78. Patrick Darling, *The Myth of Overpopulation*, London: Institute of Economic Affairs, in press.

79. Darling cites the following studies: P. Hill, *Rural Hausa: A Village and a Setting*, Cambridge University Press (1972); Michael Mortimore, 'Shifting Sands and Human Sorrow: Social Response to Drought and Desertification', *Desertification Control Bulletin* No. 14, United Nations Environment Programme (1987); Michael Mortimore, 'Resilience in semi-arid Africa', MS for Patrick Darling (ed.) *The Changing Sahara* (unpublished); Michael Mortimore, *Adapting to Drought: Farmers, Famines and Desertification in West Africa*, Cambridge University Press (1989).

80. Darling cites his own study *Farming Systems Survey Report*, KARI/ODA Crop Protection Project, Nairobi, Kenya (1992).

81. Cf. HRH Prince Philip, op.cit.

82. Jonathon Porritt, 'Stewards of the Earth', op.cit., p. 44.

83. From Frank Barnaby (ed.), *The Gaia Peace Atlas*, London: Pan Books (1988) p. 161.

84. Sean McDonagh, *The Greening of the Church*, London: Geoffrey Chapman (1990) p. 50.

85. Garrett Hardin, op.cit, p.175.

86. Paul and Anne Ehrlich, *Earth*, London: Thames Methuen (1987) p. 59.

87. From Paul Ciotti, 'Fear of Fusion: What If It Works?', *Los Angeles*

Times (19 April 1989) Section V pp. 1-2. Quoted in Virginia Postrel, 'The Green Road to Serfdom', *Reason* (April 1990) p. 28.

88. Ibid.

89. Dixy Lee Ray with Lou Guzzo, *Trashing the Planet: How Science Can Help Us Deal with Acid Rain, Depletion of the Ozone, and Nuclear Waste (Among Other Things)*, Washington: Regnery Gateway (1990); republished in paperback by HarperCollins, New York (1992).

90. A.J. Lebrun, *War on Hunger*, Agency for International Development (1969); quoted in Thomas H. Jukes, 'Insecticides in Health, Agriculture and the Environment', *Naturwissenschaften* 61 (1974) pp. 6-16.

91. Rachel Carson, *Silent Spring*, Boston: Houghton Mifflin (1962).

92. Stephen Fox, *John Muir and His Legacy: The American Conservation Movement*, Boston: Little, Brown and Company (1981) p. 292.

93. *The Place of DDT in Operations against Malaria and Other Vector-Borne Diseases*, Off. Rec. World Health Organisation No. 190, Geneva (April 1971); quoted in Thomas H. Jukes, op. cit.

94. The evidence against the point of view that DDT damaged birds is reviewed by Thomas Jukes, op. cit.; the evidence for the case against DDT can be found in Tom J. Cade (ed.) *Peregrine Falcon Populations: Their Management and Recovery* Boise, Idaho: The Peregrine Fund (1988).

95. World Health Organisation, op. cit.

96. Quoted in Elizabeth Whelan, *Toxic Terror*, Ottawa, Illinois: Jameson Books (1985) p. 85.

97. Elizabeth Whelan, op.cit., footnote p. 67.

98. Quoted in Groen, Smit and Eizsvogel (eds.) *The Discipline of Curiosity*, New York: Elsivir (1990) p. 43.

99. Dixy Lee Ray and Lou Guzzo, *Trashing the Planet*, op.cit., p. 82.

100. Sean McDonagh, op.cit., p. 111.

101. Arthur Kay 'When Green is Red' *Calvinism Today* (January 1991).

102. Jonathon Porritt, 'Stewards of the Earth', op.cit., p. 46.

103. E.Calvin Beisner, 'Environmentalism or Stewardship? What is the Christian's responsibility?', *Proceedings from the Seminar on Ecology and Religion* (April 30 - May 1 1993) Washington: Competitive Enterprise Institute, p. 43

104. Edward Echlin, 'Population Theology', text of a paper given to the First World Optimum Population Congress, held in Cambridge (9-11 August 1993).

105. Arthur Kay, op. cit.

106. Don Hinrichsen, 'Coasts under pressure', *People and the Planet*, Vol 3 No 1, London: International Planned Parenthood Federation (1994) p. 7.

107. Alexander Volokh, 'How Green Is Our Valley?', *Reason* (March 1995) p. 59.

108. Quoted in Robert Nelson, 'Unoriginal Sin: The Judeo-Christian Roots of Ecotheology', *Policy Review* 53 (Summer) pp. 52-59.

109. Simone Weil, *Notebooks*, tr. A. Wills, London: Routledge and Kegan Paul (1956) vol II, p. 423.

110. R. Jeffers, 'An Extinct Vertebrate' in R. I. Scott (ed.) *What Odd Expedients, and Other Poems*, Hamden CT: Archon Books (1981) p. 54.

111. Stephen R.L. Clark, *How to Think about the Earth: Philosophical and Theological Models for Ecology*, London: Mowbray (1993) p. 42.

112. P. J. O'Rourke, *All the Trouble in the World: The Lighter Side of Overpopulation, Famine, Ecological Disaster, Ethnic Hatred, Plague, and Poverty*, New York: Atlantic Monthly Press (1994) p. 121.

113. Dave Foreman, 'The Destruction of Wilderness', *Earth First!* (21 December 1989) p. 20, quoted in Robert Nelson, 'Environmental Calvinism: The Judeo-Christian Roots of Eco-Theology' in Roger E. Meiners and Bruce Yandle (eds.) *Taking the Environment Seriously*, Lanham, Maryland:Rowman and Littlefield (1993) p. 239.

114. David Graber, 'Mother Nature as a Hothouse Flower', *Los Angeles Times Book Review* (22 October 1989). Quoted in Virginia Postrel, 'The Green Road to Serfdom', *Reason* (April 1990).

115. Norman Myers and Julian Simon, *Scarcity or Abundance: A Debate on the Environment*, New York: W.W. Norton (1994) pp. 103 and 104.

116. Quoted in Greg Easterbrook, 'Everything You Know About the Environment is Wrong', *The New Republic* (30 April 1990) p. 18; and in Robert James Bidinotto, 'Environmentalism: Freedom's Foe for the '90s', *The Freeman* (November 1990) p. 414.

117. Quoted in M. John Fayhee, 'Earth First! and Foremost', *Backpacker* (September 1988) p.21, also in Robert James Bidinotto, op. cit., p. 414.

118. Virginia Postrel, 'The Green Road to Serfdom', *Reason* (April 1990) pp. 22-28.

CHAPTER THREE

Greens and Animals

Joseph Kirwan

Those who propose that animals have rights have a deficient appreciation of the basic forms of human good. At the root of their contention is the conception that human good consists essentially in sentience; for it is only sentience that is common to human beings and the animals which are said to have rights ... Even if we consider the bodily human goods, and those simply as experienced, we see that the quality of this experience is very different from a merely animal consciousness, since it is experienced as expressive of decision, choice, reflectiveness, commitment, as fruition of purpose or of self-discipline or self-abandonment, and as an action of a responsible personality. The basic human goods are not abstract forms, such as 'life' or 'conscious life': they are good as aspects of the flourishing of a person

John Finnis, *Natural Law and Natural Rights*[1]

What a Piece of Work is Man

There is a 'danger of taking ourselves as being more important than the rest of God's creation' according to the authors of *Faith & The Environment*, a leaflet published by the World Wide Fund for Nature (WWF).

To that judgement the Christian must reply that God thinks us so important that he sent his Son to become one of us, to take upon Himself our human nature, to live the life of a man, to die the death of a man.

> The Word was made flesh,
> he lived among us,
> and we saw his glory
>
> Jn.1:14

102

So said Christ's beloved disciple John, a man who saw his Master die on a cross, was a witness to his resurrection, and watched his ascent into heaven. It is that Christ, God made man, who enjoins us to have so high an opinion of our worth as to trust always in His provision for us. The birds are provided for, he says, 'and how much more are you worth than the birds!' (Lk.12:24).

The Greens will have none of this; they do not accept the words of Christ. They believe that man is of rather less worth than a bird because whereas a bird fits into the world, man is often engaged in activities that threaten to destroy it. When man is compared with a bird, is not man the inferior being?

Nevertheless, while Greens blame man bitterly for his destructiveness, they allow that he has rights, although they would claim that these are limited by the rights which animals have.

In this the Greens are mistaken. They are mistaken both about the rights they imagine animals to have, and those they claim for themselves as men.

Can Animals have Rights ?

The rights they talk about are not derived from man-made laws. They are thought to be of a kind that man-made laws should recognise as already existing. The term for rights of that sort is *natural right*, used originally as a translation of the Latin term *ius naturale*. They are so-called because they emerge from the nature of the person or creature possessing them. Thus, when the Greens say that animals (or some of them) have the same (or some of the same) rights as men possess, they are saying that, in the relevant respects, the animals that have them are of the same nature as men; or the other way around, that man is an animal; or at least is in some relevant respects similar to, or in the likeness of, some animals. This has theological implications, but let us stay for a while with the philosophy. If we are to speak of animal rights we have to examine the history of the term *natural right* or *ius naturale*.

What are Rights ?

The Latin word *ius* in its origins means a 'bond' or a 'tie'. Thus the Romans spoke of *ius amicitiae* (the bond of friendship) and of *ius necessitudinis* (the bond of a relationship). Hence in law *ius* came to have the primary meaning of 'duty'. Only secondarily did it mean 'right'. Lewis and Short's Latin Dictionary defines *ius* as: 'that which is binding or obligatory; that which is of its nature right; justice; duty'. The great code of law of the Emperor Justinian says: 'the rules of *ius* are these: to live becomingly; to harm no man; to give to every man that which is his'.

It is worth noticing that this last is the definition of justice that St Thomas Aquinas gives in his *Summa Theologiae* (2a 2ae Q. 58 art. 1): 'justice is the habit whereby one renders to every man that which is his' (*Justitia est habitus secundum quem ... ius suum unicuique tribuit*). Elsewhere Aquinas quotes the 2nd century jurist Celsus that *ius* is the art of the good and equitable.

Lewis and Short also quote from Cicero that *ius* is found at the roots of human society. This was the view of the fourth century BC philosopher Aristotle: 'it is a characteristic of man that he alone has any sense of good and evil, of just and unjust, and the like; and it is the association of living beings who have this sense that makes a family and a state'.[2] Because of that, Aristotle added, men are impelled to live in society even when they have no need of mutual help. Man's impulsion to live in civil societies comes not only from his need to make life possible, but also to make the good life possible, i.e. one in which virtue can be sought after.

Thus the emphasis of *ius* is on duty to perform rather than right to enjoy. As John Finnis points out, *ius* in Roman law 'might be a burden, not a benefit — let alone a power of liberty of choice'.[3] In *ius naturale* duty comes first. Right flows from duty. It is because men have duties that they have rights.

Rights and Right Reason

In the work of the fourteenth century Oxford philosopher William of Ockham (sometimes called Occam) we find a movement away from the primacy of duty in his definition of *ius naturale* as a 'legitimate power'.[4] However, he retained the balance by his insistence that this power had to accord with *recta ratio* — right reason. It is this right reason that provides the standard of morality, i.e. of duty. In this he followed Aristotle in defining right reason as consisting in the mean between excess and deficiency: to insist on taking more or less than fits a case is to behave irrationally. Any man's right is defined by his duty to see that, as far as in him lies, all men can enjoy the benefits of society, offering not only access to means of subsistence but also opportunities for cultural, moral and religious development.

All of this philosophical reasoning is in conformity with what we know of human history and have gathered from archaeological investigations. This is man's experience, despite numerous and heart-rending setbacks. Furthermore, to Christians, it defines the conduct that is consistent with right behaviour. There have always been political or civil associations with these ends in view, even where there did not exist what we would now call a city or a state. Even the most primitive tribes known to us have or had complex social relationships and codes of behaviour designed to facilitate duty/right relationships.

Nowhere is there evidence of such relationships or a like development among animals. The most primitive tribal codes are more complex than any that can be found outside humanity. A pride of lions, a herd of elephants, or even a group of high apes has nothing to compare with human codes. It is only with men that *ius naturale* and *recta ratio* are found.

Despite these established truths, people who speak of 'rights' today generally mean something quite different from what philosophers of the last 2,000 years have understood by *ius*; so that today's 'natural right' has a meaning far removed from the traditional meaning of *ius naturale*. There has been a shift in the concept of what it means to be human. The process of change took time, but by the seventeenth century, in England at least, it seems to have been completed.

'Solitary, Poor, Nasty, Brutish, and Short'

Thomas Hobbes' book *Leviathan* marked a turning point in man's view of himself and of his place in the world. It was not that Hobbes threw out all that had gone before; what he did was to open a door to let in a draught which blew much that was rational into confusion.

He continued to use the old term *ius naturale*, but the meaning he gave to it was utterly different from that which had been understood by Cicero, Aquinas and Ockham. In his use of it he divorced right from duty, denied man's social nature, and gave to natural right an entirely individualistic meaning.

The man of Hobbes' theorising is solitary. He is moved only by a passionate desire for his own individual security in an utterly hostile world. When he enters into a relationship with others it is entirely from his own selfish interest. There is no society, only a mob of individuals huddled together in fear of a perpetual state of war in which each is more likely to be trodden down than to come out on top.

Hobbes' own definition of his 'right of nature' (which he persisted in calling *ius naturale*) was 'the liberty which each man hath, to use his own power, as he will himself, for the preservation of his own nature: that is to say, his own life; and consequently of doing anything which in his own judgement, and reason, he shall conceive to be the aptest thereunto'.[5]

Hobbes was aware that, in the absence of what he called 'external impediments' (because his man had no brake of his own) this individual liberty for everyone must lead to a state of affairs in which:

> ... there will be no place for industry; ... no culture of the earth; no navigation; ... no commodious building; ... no knowledge of the face of the earth; no account of time; no arts; no letters; no society ... continual fear, and danger of violent death; and the life of man, solitary, poor, nasty, brutish and short.[6]

Here, one might say, is a picture of animal life in the wild, were it not that animals have no capacity for industry or culture or letters and, more importantly, are equipped with built-in brakes that prevent them from preying on members of their own species, and make them content to take from those on which they do prey only as much as is needed for the day. Hobbes' man, a creature without brakes, is the worst enemy of his own kind. His appetite for destruction is without limit for, says Hobbes, 'in such a condition every man has a right to everything, even to another's body'.[7] Surely, we must say, in such a condition the word 'right' is without meaning.

Manifestly we do not live in such a world, nor, it must be supposed, did Hobbes believe that we did. In his view, man had reason and judgement enough to escape from the consequences of the 'rights of nature' by making pacts with solitary creatures like himself. These would take the form: 'If you undertake to give up this or that liberty, I shall do the same'. Thus each one could buy a precarious truce in which he is ever fearful, watchful and ready to revert to war, which might be said to be his natural condition. Such pacts create no moral obligation. It is necessity that drives the solitary individuals into making them, and the same necessity that compels them to abide by them, as far as others will allow.

There is nothing here for animal rights, or even for rights without meaning. Nevertheless, a recent author has suggested that since:

> In line with Hobbes' thinking ... whatever any human being does in the state of nature — i.e. in the wild, outside civil society — he has the natural right to do ... there is no reason why the Hobbesian idea could not be extended to all animals, human or not.[8]

Human, perhaps, if man is an animal that lacks in-built brakes; but animals proper, no. Hobbes is concerned with man's difficulties in living in the same world as his fellows. Animals — real animals — do not have such a nature. Their patterns of behaviour are fixed. Herbivores eat grass; carnivores eat herbivores and other carnivores; scavengers eat what others leave. Animals have no need for rights among themselves.

Hobbes and Animal Rights

As for rights between animals and Hobbes' man, Hobbes himself ruled that out. While his men in the state of nature could procure some precarious rights by entering into pacts with one another, between men and animals this could not happen. Animals 'not understanding our speech, they understand not, nor accept, any translation of right'.[9]

This can be said: the only animals that might be said to have found refuge from the life which is 'poor, nasty, brutish and short' that Hobbes allows men in the state of nature, are those that have been domesticated by man or are systematically hunted by him. They are at man's disposal, they are slaughtered by him when he wills, but meantime he offers them security. This is not, one supposes, what animal rights advocates have in mind.

Animal Duties

So, to sum up, if we speak of rights in the full sense, i.e. *ius* = duty, animals, having no duty, have no right. Nor is the right without duty for which Hobbes argued (and which many people today seem to be claiming for themselves) available to animals. In fact the impediment to such a right goes deeper than that of which Hobbes wrote. It is because they cannot think, having no consciousness of their own existence, that animals lack ability to communicate ideas. An animal cannot stand apart from itself and contemplate its own activities, give them purpose and so make them its acts. It is a dumb creature, in the literal and the colloquial American sense. It can neither speak nor think. It is not responsible.

Man is responsible. He can think. He can know what he is doing. Knowing, he can choose. To the extent that he is denied opportunity to choose he is treated as subhuman, as active merely, not acting. To be human is to have the power to act; i.e. to know what he intends to do, is doing, has done. Thus man alone works. That is his distinctive mark, as Pope John Paul II has pointed out in his encyclical letter *Laborem Exercens* (*On Human Work*).

The Scale of Importance in Nature

However, the advocates of animal rights are not concerned with duty, nor does it bother them that animals, being without reason, cannot make binding pacts with men. They appeal to the Darwinian theory of evolution — that the history of the physical world is one of development from lower to higher forms of existence, so that the later are better, in some relevant sense, than the earlier. The earlier forms of life are simpler, the later are more complex. In relation to the question of rights, it does not matter whether or not the theory of evolution can be taken to be established. What does matter is the assertion that the greater the complexity of the creature, the higher it has to be placed on the scale of intrinsic values (a scale not made by man but one which he is capable of recognising) of such a sort that rights begin to emerge at the upper end. Creatures that man is somehow obliged to admit to have rights in some degree will be seen to have them *in their own right*.

There seems to be a lack of logic in this application of evolutionary theory. As Aristotle (no mean naturalist) pointed out long ago, the simplest form of creature is perfectly adapted to the place in the world in which it has existence:

Even creatures that do not charm the senses disclose to intellectual

108

perception the nature (*physis*) which designs them and give immense pleasure to all who, in studying them, can work back to causes and be true philosophers .. ... Therefore, we must not recoil with childish aversion from examination of the humblest of animals. In every work of nature some marvel resides. We ought then to proceed without distaste to the consideration of every animal in the conviction that each has its share of nature (*physis*) and of beauty. For in the works of nature it is not chance that rules, but in the highest degree purpose. The end for which a creature is shaped and produced is a form of the beautiful.[10]

As that world changes, of course, creatures adapted to it disappear and new forms of animal life emerge, adapted to the new as the others were to the old. The later are not necessarily intrinsically better than the old. The dinosaurs, generally regarded as creatures, like Pooh Bear, of very little brain, had a dominant position among other creatures over an extremely long stretch of time. They could not live in today's world; but today's 'successes' could not have lived in theirs. On what ground could it be said that the animals we know today have greater value or importance than those of an earlier age? More to the point, perhaps, on what ground can it be said that today a lion is of more value or importance than a limpet?

This hierarchy of values among animals (and other things) is not held only by animal rights advocates. Tibor Machan, the author of *Do Animals Have Rights* (in which he decides that they do not) argues: 'while it makes no sense to evaluate as good or bad such things as planets or rocks or pebbles — except as they may relate to human purposes — when it comes to plants and animals the process of evaluation commences very naturally indeed'. There is, he says, 'a scale of importance in nature and among all the various kinds of being'.[11]

One might ask, why begin evaluation with plants and animals? Why should not rocks and pebbles be evaluated as good or bad, better or worse, in themselves, without reference to human needs or notions? They exist in great variety and vary greatly in age. It might be objected that plants and animals have life and that rocks and pebbles merely exist. In the face of what we know now of molecular structure of solids we might begin to question whether there is anything in this world that is truly inanimate.

Be that as it may, we might ask why plants are ranked below animals in importance. They have life, indubitably, yet nobody speaks up for vegetable rights, although G.K. Chesterton did once ask vegetarians to pay heed to the anguished cry of the carrot as it was wrenched from its bed.

It might, perhaps, be said that animals have greater value *in themselves* than plants because vegetable life is earlier than animal life, but is that true? Can vegetable life exist without animal life? The natural world is a harmony of inter-related species. In what sense can we speak of a hierarchy dependent on or linked with time?

Nevertheless, there is said to be a scale of importance in nature. It would seem to be impossible, intellectually, to hold that anything or anyone (other than God) can have value or importance other than to someone or something else. Animal rights activists seem to accept this tacitly. They speak of a 'hierarchical structure in nature', such that 'the level of importance or value may be noted to move from the inanimate to the animate world, culminating, as far as we now know, with human life'.[12] Man is part of the scale, though on top. Therefore, positions on the scale cannot be assigned by him. Nature does that. All that he can do is read the scale.

So runs the argument summarised by Machan. It does seem odd. Men habitually assign values to things and creatures, as they seem always to have done, with reference largely, if not entirely, to themselves — not necessarily selfishly, often altruistically. Aristotle was probably not the first, certainly by no means the last, to observe that men are of their nature social.

We have to ask, what is this nature that has its own scale of value or importance, a scale observable by man but not established by him? The Shorter Oxford English Dictionary gives two definitions of nature that might be relevant to this question.

1. The creative and regulative physical power which is conceived of as operating in the physical world and as the immediate cause of its phenomena. Personified as a female being, usually with a capital 'N'.

2. The material world, or its collective objects or phenomena, the features and products of the earth itself, as contrasted with human civilisation.

A collection of objects or phenomena can hardly provide a scale of value. It is the first of these definitions which is relevant to that notion. Those who think and speak in this way ought to write Nature so, with a capital 'N'. They personify, if not deify, an idea, or perhaps an abstract noun. Only thus can it be explained why so many of them talk of Gaia, the earth goddess.

There is no lack of examples of this personification or deification of 'Nature'. At a Harvest Festival in Winchester Cathedral in 1987 the Dean appeared to express doubts as to whether or not God holds the world entirely in His own hands. Speaking at the offering of the fruits of the earth (which truly are the fruits of man's work) he said: 'As a priest, I can offer absolution from God for those sins for which we ask his forgiveness. We shall not know if Nature has forgiven us for many years to come'.[13]

Let us revert to Machan's statement about rocks, plants and animals, bearing in mind that he does not believe in animal rights but simply repeats uncritically the small change of general discussion about man and his place in the world. He says:

> If man were uniquely important, that would mean that one could not assign any value to plants or non-humans apart from their relationship to human beings.[14]

The root of the case for animal rights lies there. Its advocates do not believe that man is unique. That is why the notion of animal rights lies quite outside the Christian (or Jewish or Muslim) view of the world of God's creation and of man's place in it. As Joseph Fuchs says in his *Natural Law*:

> In man as willed and created by God not everything is 'nature'. That is to say *not everything that he is derives from his composite being as body and soul* ... Man in his total existence is and always has been directed positively to a supernatural end. It is from this fact that he receives his significance ... The word *natura* means man as he was in the beginning, deriving as it does from *nasci* which means 'to be born'. It follows that in this sense the supernatural is not accidental to man. It belongs to his definition essentially ... As distinct from the supernatural, nature is but a part of that total reality which is man and which we know exclusively from Revelation.[15]

The Paganism of Animal Rights

The animal rights movement is pagan. Its advocates give no credence to — and indeed either implicitly or explicitly deny — the gulf which lies between man and the merely natural world. They do not recognise man for what he is. To quote Aquinas:

> Things are likened to God, first and most generally insofar as they are; secondly insofar as they are alive; thirdly and lastly insofar as they have discernment and intelligence. It is these latter, as Augustine says, which are so close to likeness to God that there is nothing greater in all creation.[16]

It is in the teeth of this that animal rights advocates persist in maintaining that man is an animal at the top of a pyramid composed of other animal and vegetable things (*entia*) which differ in degrees of natural value but not at all in essence. That only man can think does not disturb them because they set but little value, if any, on capacity to reason, judge, plan, decide. It is enough, to quote Machan (who, let us remind ourselves, does not himself believe that animals have rights) that animals 'can feel pain and can enjoy themselves'.[17]

It may be that this is so, but if it be so it can be of importance only if it is true also that the good for both man and beast consists essentially in sentience; for, as Finnis remarks, 'it is only sentience that is common to human beings and the animals that are said to have rights'.[18]

The elevation of feeling goes to the heart of the matter. The mistake about man's good flows from the utter ignorance of the kind of being man is. That, in its turn, could flow from a belief that there is no purpose in the world, except in 'Nature'. They apply to man what is certainly true of animals: they have no purpose that is known to themselves. They are active: they do not act. They are driven entirely by their own instincts. When an animal is hungry it seeks the particular sort of food ordained for its species. When it is sleepy, it sleeps as, where and when the instincts peculiar to its species impel it. Animals seek sexual release according to the patterns built into them. They care for their offspring in the same way; and once that species-directed job is done, they take no further interest. At no time is there any willed intention.

As Finnis has shown so well, man is the exception on every count.

Each makes his own patterns of behaviour and changes them as he judges his circumstances require. It is this characteristic of purposefulness that reveals man as outside all other manner of earthly being; as being, in fact, in essence outside it. He is the only creature whose end is not death but a purpose.

It becomes abundantly clear that a Christian cannot consistently believe in animal rights. Greenery puts man, whose nature God takes to himself in Christ Jesus, Mary's son, below the level of the animals (or, in Greenspeak, the non-human animals). Animals fit in with Nature, while men persist in manipulating it, using its laws to change what is given to them, seeking their own advantage, sometimes making mistakes and doing damage. Men get above themselves and hardly deserve to survive.

It is not accidental that a characteristic of Greenery is that its practitioners denigrate, and even hate, mankind. Yet they do seem to perceive, in a twisted way, that man is something Nature is not. Why else should they look to men to recognise, and make real, the rights they claim for animals?

However they do not know, or will not admit, the truth about man — that he cannot give to animals rights which God gave to him when charging him with the task of subduing the earth. Man cannot accept that animals have either active or passive rights, because neither the one nor the other exists for them.

This does not mean that men have no duties with regard to animals. However these duties are not *to* animals, for if man had such duties animals would have rights against man. Man's duties are to God, and they are the other side of man's rights. Man's duties with regard to the rest of earthly creation form the point of the Genesis story of the creation of mankind in the persons of Adam and Eve.

Yet not all Christians perceive this. It has been said that in his Encyclical *Sollicitudo Rei Socialis* Pope John Paul II concedes that men must respect the creatures of the world, not because failure to do so would result in undesirable consequences, but because they have a right to be respected. For the reasons I have been advancing in the forgoing argument, this is something the Pope could not say.

As its opening words indicate, the encyclical is concerned with society. Animals are not social. The concern, then, is with human society. It is not with animals or plants or clean air and water or conservation of resources, except insofar as the manner in which man uses these things has a bearing on his growth in humanity in his journey through this mortal life to death and judgement.

Sollicitudo Rei Socialis was written to celebrate the twentieth anniversary of the encyclical letter of Pope Paul VI, *Populorum Progressio*, on the development of mankind. These two encyclicals both look back, in their turn, to Pope Leo XIII's encyclical *Rerum Novarum*, on the condition of the working classes, which was published in 1891. This might reasonably be called the fountainhead of the Church's teaching on the moral problems which have arisen in a world that is driven into rapid and far-reaching change by technical and technological advances. Man's ingenuity has unleashed forces which he finds it difficult to control. The problems that directly concern the Church are moral and theological. Questions of ecology are incidental; being technical, they are not within the Church's competence.

Are Animals Creatures or Things?

Unfortunately, people who are inclined to look favourably on the claims of animal rights advocates have been somewhat led astray by the poor translation of the original Latin text of *Sollicitudo Rei Socialis* into English. Thus, at para. 34, the English version says:

> Nor can the moral character of development exclude respect for the beings which constitute the natural world, which the ancient Greeks — alluding precisely to the order which distinguishes it — called 'the cosmos'. Such realities also demand respect.[19]

The word *being* has proved to be a stumbling block, as also has the word *demand*. At least one commentator has turned *beings* into *creatures*, as well he might, given that he thinks animals have rights. The English version is a translation from the Italian, which might mislead the unwary. However, the authentic version is the Latin.

Beings is a rendering of the Italian *esseri*. This can mean *beings* but it can also mean *essences*, *existences*, *entities* or *realities*. The English translator made the wrong choice. The Latin text has *entia*, which simply means *things*. This conclusion is re-inforced by the remark in the succeeding sub-paragraph, in which we are told to become more conscious of the fact that we cannot make use of *these things* arbitrarily without paying the penalty. *These things* are animate and inanimate — trees, animals and natural elements. It would be odd indeed to call a tree a creature or even a being. A tree worshipper might, but then tree worship is not rational.

So also with *demands* in this context. The Italian is *esigoni*, a verb which, used in relation to things, means *requires*. A thing cannot make demands. *Requires* puts the emphasis where it belongs: the human being has to his intelligence and his good will to perceive what is needed in the circumstances. *Demand* puts the emphasis on the thing: it is telling the human being what he has to do.

These may look like pettifogging points but they are not. So far-reaching and so deeply-rooted is the belief that animals have rights that shoddy translation can cause much damage through misunderstanding and conscious or subconscious bad teaching. In the same section John Paul II is at pains to emphasise that it is the moral law that is decisive for man. The laws of biology — a quite different sense of the word 'law' — form but the raw material, so to speak, on which man's reason has to work. The right objectively moral decision is unlikely to arise out of biological ignorance, and that applies particularly to the Greens, who often reveal extraordinary ignorance of biology.

Vegetarianism and the Bible

Christian Greens are also sometimes guilty of making selective use of the Bible. When faced with the fact that God gave to man in the beginning dominion over the earth and all that is in it, they quibble about the word *dominion*. It can be said that Christian exegetes have consistently held this to mean what a farmer means by *good husbandry*. That is to say that whoever has control of anything has a duty to use it in such wise that those coming after him are not prevented from enjoying dominion. And, as any good husbandman knows, such caring and careful use does not exclude weeding out, cutting down, burning and killing. Indeed it may very well require of him any or all of these acts.

Some Christian Greens cite the Book of Genesis in support of their view that killing for food is forbidden by the Bible:

God said, 'See, I give you all the seed-bearing plants that are upon the

115

whole earth, and all the trees with seed-bearing fruit; this shall be your food. To all wild beasts, all birds of heaven and all living reptiles on the earth I give all the foliage of plants for food'.

Genesis 1:29-30

On this passage is built a case for vegetarianism.

Leaving aside the fact that carnivorous animals are not equipped to feed on grass and seeds and leaves, we can trump Genesis 1:29-30 with Genesis 9:3 in which God speaks to Noah and his sons after the flood and tells them that 'Every living and crawling thing shall provide food for you, no less than the foliage of plants'. It might be profitable to confront this apparent contradiction.

The Jews of the Old Testament were meat eaters, though particular about which kinds of meat they ate. Christ our Lord ate meat though, being a poor man, probably not much or often. He certainly ate the Paschal lamb. After his resurrection he ate broiled fish with his disciples (John 21:9-13). It is to be supposed that fish counts as meat in this context, as fish is neither vegetable nor mineral.

So also with Peter. The bundle let down to him on the roof at Caesarea (Acts 10:9-16) did not contain peas and parsnips, but all manner of animals and birds. The voice that spoke to him said 'Now, Peter, kill and eat'. (The Knox version gives a more graphic rendering: 'Rise up, Peter, lay about thee and eat'.)

The Jewish niceness about what sorts of meat could be eaten was removed in an extraordinary way; eat whatever you like, kill and eat anything and everything. That was the rule for Peter and, if we accept the authenticity of the Bible, it is the rule for us. We are sent back to Noah. We are not to be squeamish about killing.

It is easy to use the Bible to our own destruction. Peter was told that he could lawfully eat any kind of meat he chose, but that did not mean that it would always and everywhere be right for him to do so. We must keep in mind Paul's admonition to the Romans:

> ... the kingdom of God does not mean eating or drinking this or that; it means righteousness and peace and joy brought by the Holy Spirit ... Of course all food is clean, but it becomes evil if by eating it you make somebody else fall away ... You are certainly not free to eat what you like if that means the downfall of someone for whom Christ died.

Rom. 14:17,20,15

This is an admonition to which both meat-eaters and vegetarians would do well to give heed.

We know that the Bible is to be read in the light of the tradition handed down by the Apostles, of which it forms a major part. The churches that hold to that tradition, East and West, have no truck with a prohibition on killing animals for food.

Do Animals Feel Pain?

To eat man must kill living creatures, some of which, according to proponents of theories of animal rights, have rights that men ought to recognise. Such killing appears to entail pain. Reference has already been made to Tibor Machan's remark: 'we know that animals can feel pain and can enjoy themselves'.[20] But do we?

It is all too easy to use language in a confusing way, transferring our experience of life to animals because their physical reactions to certain stimuli look much like our own. Such resemblance between their reactions and ours is to be expected, given that they and we have the same or very similar nervous systems. That at least seems to be true of what are called the higher animals, although even a worm or an eel will exhibit signs of what, with us, would be called distress. That animals should have disagreeable sensations when damaged is part of the cosmic economy: creatures that did not have consciousness of the difference between safe and unsafe stimuli would not last long in the world. The question is not that but rather: do animals feel pain as we feel pain? Do they experience joy as we do? Are they conscious of either or both as we are?

A significant difference between man and the animals is that he alone in the earthly creation is conscious of his own existence. He can, so to speak, stand outside himself and be aware of his body as distinct from his psyche. It is in this way that man is radically different from the animals. An animal is a unit: it is a body. Man is a unity: he is body-soul, and the soul is rational. This being so, it is not unreasonable to argue that the human experience of pain is different from that of the animal.

In connection with the propaganda for animal rights it is important also to recognise that the infliction of pain is a morally neutral act. What matters is the purpose of the act. The mother who pots her baby uses force, and the baby often objects strongly. The mother who slaps the hand of the child who persists in trying to touch a hot plate inflicts pain. Medical treatment often causes pain. Uses such as these are licit because the pain is inflicted as a necessary element in action taken for the sufferer's good.

Sometimes pain inflicted on an animal (assuming for the moment that an animal can feel pain as we do) will be for the benefit of the animal. More often than not, such pain (if it is indeed what we know as pain) is entirely for our benefit and not for that of the animal. House training a puppy requires treatment that the puppy certainly does not like. Breaking a horse to wear harness, or to be ridden, or to answer to the reins, involves treatment that is not to the animal's liking. Actions such as these are licit because we stand to an animal as user to used. Had oxen never been trained to the plough, mankind would not have risen above a bare subsistence economy. Had no animal been domesticated — and the process must have been exceedingly disagreeable to animals taken from the wild — man could hardly have survived.

To repeat an essential point: from the beginning the man to animal relationship is that of user to used. So, we should not be concerned that killing for food could or does cause pain to the creatures we kill. That it does not benefit the animals killed is a matter of no moral importance.

To summarise: philosophically it is illicit to argue from human experience to what looks like similar animal experience. Second, theologically, in the history of the Jewish and Christian people of God, there is no trace of condemnation of meat-eating with its attendant killing. Inept philosophy and perverted theology came very late upon the scene. It comes strongly now when belief in the God of Abraham, Isaac and Jacob is largely abandoned, even by many who still say they are Christian.

Dominion of man over man is licit only when it is for the common good, that is, a good which both orderer and ordered share.[21] The case of man's dominion over creatures is different. The dominator of an animal only has to consider human good.

The Use and Misuse of Animals

This does not mean that we have no duty to God in our treatment of animals. This question comes to the fore in considering the use of animals for experiments. Pain caused (or apparently caused) to the animal is permissible provided that the benefit to mankind can reasonably be reckoned to be sufficiently great. It is much to be doubted if experimentation on animals for cosmetic purposes could pass that test.

There is more reason to be astonished at the uproar over 'intensive' farming. Every domesticated animal is subjected to what, for a human, would be a sentence of life imprisonment, be the prison open, or high-security or anything in between. All farming, from the viewpoint of the wild, is intensive, although some methods are more so than others. The purpose of all farming is food for people, not pleasure for the animals so-used. Whether or not animals find it irksome — and one cannot but see that in most cases the irksomeness is in the minds of the observers who project their human feelings upon animals which are incapable of experiencing them — men do well to farm.

Bearing in mind that animals exist for our good, one cannot but answer that if the meat, eggs etc. are wholesome food, we can assume that the animals from which these good things come are not misused.

That is the point, both philosophically and theologically. We ought to *use* animals for our good. Between ourselves and God we have always to give an account of what we do with whatever he puts in our care. We may not *abuse* anything, animate or inanimate, because in so doing we estrange ourselves from him who trusts us with the care of creatures and of the earth's resources. What we do with an animal is licit if we are thereby enabled to feed the hungry, heal the sick, clothe the naked, provide opportunity for men to work and supply the things that increase the well-being of God's children.

That rule is safe. Anyone who follows it will not *abuse* or *misuse* an animal or any other thing in God's creation. This can be put another way. A man is *abusing* or *misusing* an animal if what he does with it makes him a worse man. It is always man's good that is at stake.

Aquinas provides what might be considered a footnote to that argument. He teaches that an animal has no good of its own, properly speaking. In his introduction to Volume 34 of the Blackfriars edition of the *Summa Theologiae*, Thomas Gilby observes that 'man is called to the highest good and beyond, for our friendship is invited by God as revealing himself to himself and for himself, not only as the object in which our thoughts and affections about his creatures culminate and are integrated. It is about *agape*, the highest loving men can be made capable of'.[22] No animal is capable of that; no animal can share in it. They are not made like us, in God's image and likeness. God loves them as he does all that he keeps in being, but they cannot love God.

Puppy Love

This leads to the question of man's love of animals, on which the Greens put great emphasis. Now, love is a slippery word. It is used in many contexts to indicate many different kinds of relationships. We have to ask, what is the nature of our relationship with animals ?

I once met a woman who said that she loved a particular tree. One can see what she meant — or, rather, would have meant had she given thought to the connection between her feelings and her words. Contemplating the tree she was struck by its beauty. That beauty drew a response from her. She, as a creature made in the image and likeness of God, could not but respond to the beautiful things in the world that God has given us. Whether or not she knew it, her 'love' for the tree was her response to God's goodness in making it and endowing her with the capacity for 'loving' it. I write 'loving' so, because love is primarily a matter of mind and will. Feeling is involved because we are sentient as well as rational beings. Our affections, our emotional responses, are connected with love, but they are not themselves love. To discover what love is we have to look to theology and philosophy. For much of what follows I shall be drawing primarily on Aristotle's *Nicomachean Ethics* Book VIII, and St. Thomas Aquinas' *Summa Theologiae* IIa IIae QQ.23-25.

According to both men, love is fully realised, most truly real, when it can properly be called friendship. This is so because friendship is the mutual exchange of good will. Perhaps we should say good willing or, as Aquinas puts it: 'when we so love another as to will what is good for him'. If two men are on familiar terms, get on well together, are helpful to one another, but each is habitually seeking whatever he can get out of the relationship, the love between them is not friendship but desire.

The highest form of friendship is 'a sharing of man with God by his sharing his happiness with us'. It is that kind of friendship that Aquinas calls charity — a use of the word that is far removed from the contemporary one.

The friendship of man with man is also charity when each loves the other by seeking the other's good, which is communion with God. It follows that no irrational creature can be loved from charity. As Aristotle has said, a man can have no true friendship with a bottle of wine, however much he may love drinking it; nor, Aquinas has added, with a horse, however much he may admire it and love riding it. In neither case is there a 'good' to which there can be a rational response. There are three reasons for this.

First, friendship means that we will the good of our friends, but an irrational creature cannot have good in the proper sense of the word, for good, says Aquinas, is the prerogative of the rational creature, which by its own free will can use the good and be master of it. An animal is not rational. It only has a sensual life and therefore cannot know the relationship between ends and means. That is why, for example, birds of a particular species always make nests to an identical pattern. They are programmed; man is not.

Secondly, friendship is founded on some community of life, whereas irrational creatures can have no share in human life, which is of its nature rational. It is only by way of metaphor that we can speak of friendship among animals or between men and animals.

Thirdly, charity is based on a sharing in eternal happiness. Irrational creatures are incapable of this.

However, adds Aquinas, animals can be loved from charity as good things we wish others to have, in that out of charity we want them to be kept for God's honour and man's service. 'Thus does God love them for charity.'

Nature Deified

Aristotle was not a Christian, obviously, but he had a sense of the divine and of man's relationship to it. Because of that he was able to understand how man is related to all that is comprised in nature. Aquinas, a Christian saint as well as an eminently learned man, had an even fuller understanding of the relationship of man to animal.

The Greens, post-Christian, reduce man to the status of an animal and fail to explain how he makes decisions, how he changes his environment, how he comes to master all else. Most importantly, perhaps, the Greens fail to understand human love. Having, in many cases, no belief in the God of Abraham, Isaac and Jacob, they have no belief in man. Theirs is a world in which man is deracinated and nature deified.

NOTES

1. John Finnis, *Natural Law and Natural Rights*, Oxford: Clarendon Press (1980) pp. 194-5.
2. Aristotle, *The Politics* 1253 a 15-18; trans. Jowett.
3. John Finnis, op.cit., p. 209.
4. William of Ockham, *Opus nonaginta dierum*, c.14; discussed by Frederick Copleston SJ in *A History of Philosophy*, New York: Image Press, Doubleday (1962/3) Vol III, pp. 112 ff.
5. Thomas Hobbes, *Leviathan*, c.XIV, p. 145 in Collins Fount Paperbacks edition (1983).
6. Ibid., c.XIII, p. 143 in Collins edition.
7. Ibid., c.XIV, p. 146 in Collins edition.
8. Tibor Machan, *Do Animals Have Rights?*, London: Social Affairs Unit (1990) p. 6.
9. Thomas Hobbes, op.cit., c.XIV, p. 152 in Collins edition.
10. Aristotle, *Treatise of the Parts of Animals* 645a 5-26. The original Greek with a French translation and commentary is to be found in *Aristote: Les Parties des Animaux*, traduit par Pierre Louis, Collection des Universités de France, Paris (1956). An English version is to be found in W.D. Ross *Aristotle: Selections*, Oxford University Press (1927) p.175.
11. Tibor Machan, op.cit., p. 12 & p. 11.
12. Ibid., p. 13.
13. Leyla Alyanak, 'Seeds of Change: The New Harvest', *The New Road*, Bulletin of the WWF Network on Conservation and Religion, Issue 4 (January - March 1988).
14. Tibor Machan, op.cit., p. 11.
15. Joseph Fuchs, *Natural Law: A Theological Approach*, Dublin: Gill & Son (1965) pp. 43-45.
16. *Summa Theologiae*, Ia Q. 93, art .2.
17. Tibor Machan, op.cit., p. 19.
18. John Finnis, op.cit., pp. 194-195.
19. *Sollicitudo Rei Socialis: Encyclical Letter of the Supreme Pontiff John*

Paul II for the Twentieth Anniversary of Populorum Progressio, London: Catholic Truth Society (1988) p.64.

20.   Tibor Machan, op.cit., p.19.

21.   John Finnis, op.cit., p.23 cf. Aquinas *Summa Theologiae* IIa IIae, Q.58, art.9, ad.3.

22.   St Thomas Aquinas, *Summa Theologiae*, London: Eyre & Spottiswoode (1975) p.xv.

CHAPTER FOUR

A Christian Ecology
Paul Haffner

The commitment of believers to a healthy environment for everyone stems directly from their belief in God the Creator, from their recognition of the effects of personal and original sin, and from the certainty of having been redeemed in Christ. Respect for life and for the dignity of the human person extends also to the rest of creation, which is called to join man in praising God.

Pope John Paul II, *Message for World Day of Peace 1990*

The word *Oekologie* appeared around the late 1860's, proposed by the German biologist Ernst Haeckel (1834-1919), and derived from the Greek expression for house or dwelling. The notion signified a study of man's habitat in a broad sense. Since Haeckel was a fervent disciple of Darwin, the word was already born into a particular philosophical milieu and continued to gather to itself further ideological nuances during the hundred years that were to follow. However, it was only around the 1960's that the idea fully became an ideology. At the practical level, over the past century or so, the science of ecology has developed rapidly to address the problems which have arisen as a result of man's increasing ability to control and affect the natural world through the technological application of science. Among the problems which ecology currently deals with are the clearance of forests, the disappearance of various animal species and the pollution of the atmosphere, the land and the waterways. Big cities are inundated with refuse, while special difficulties are encountered in the disposal of nuclear waste. These and other problems are the result of the intervention of man in the macro-environment of nature. However, man also interferes in the genetic micro-environment of cells of living organisms, so provoking various undesirable effects. Pope John Paul II in his message for peace of 1 January 1990 declared that 'we are not yet in a position to assess the biological disturbance that could result from the unscrupulous development of new forms of plant and animal life, to say nothing of unacceptable experimentation regarding the origins of human life itself.'[1]

Science or Pseudo-Science?

Alongside the development of ecology, however, there has evolved a pseudo-science based on a reductionist view of man and his environment. In this regard, the definition of what actually constitutes the environment is an important matter. Such a definition cannot be reduced to purely physical elements, but should take into account philosophical and theological considerations. With respect to the human person, the environment cannot simply be restricted to the physical, plant or animal species which form his surroundings. Thus the environment cannot be thought of as nature in its so-called crude state, but must also include some notion of man's adaptation of nature for his own use; hence one must distinguish between the *natural* and *artificial* environment. For man, who is a unity of body and soul, the natural world is not his complete environment, but considerations of human culture must enter in. Moreover, as regards the supernatural calling of man, God and His grace must form part of man's environment. As Pope John Paul II noted in his encyclical *Centesimus Annus*, it is not only the problems of the natural environment which are important but also the 'more serious destruction of the *human environment*, something which is by no means receiving the attention it deserves'.[2] Hence, for the human being, the concept of the environment cannot be reduced to a mere biological chain of vital processes. Any discussion of the natural environment of man must clearly consider the fact that the human person is constituted of soul and body and also has relationships with other human beings. Even as a natural being, the human person can arrive at a concept of God. However it is chiefly when we consider the supernatural order that we must speak of God as the Environer of the human person.[3] These considerations of the spiritual nature of man and woman are systematically excluded by such materialistic philosophies and political systems of our day as communism in its various forms, capitalism in some of its varieties, pantheism, and ideas connected with freemasonry. It may well be noted that the three main materialistic systems of the past century have been Freudianism (in its reduction of the nature of man and woman), Darwinism (in its distorted view of evolution) and Marxism (in its erroneous socio-political analysis). These and other false philosophies have had their influence on the ideology of the ecological or Green movement.

Ecology and Morality

An adequate theology of the environment therefore involves God, the human person and nature; thus problems concerning the environment cannot be resolved in purely socio-political terms. Pope John Paul II clearly notes that the ecological crisis is a moral problem.[4] This fact is often ignored by politicians and pressure group activists who use 'ecology' as a convenient slogan to obtain credibility [5] or else as a means to promote their own materialistic ideologies. It is thus totally unacceptable to follow the approach of certain ecologists who see the solution of the crisis of man and his environment in terms of population control. Such ideological manipulations have at their root an egoistic philosophy which in fact seeks to make life more pleasurable for wealthier countries by disregarding the interests of the less well-developed nations. In such poorer states, population control will often rob towns of that very manpower which would be necessary for the development and care of the environment.

Christian Cosmology

The Christian moral system which is used to discern the just course of action in the ecological realm must itself be based on the Christian vision of the cosmos. It is clear from history that the Church possesses a strong theological tradition which respects the earth and all it contains. Saint Benedict and Saint Francis have taught us, in their different yet complementary ways, to respect God's creation. In the Benedictine tradition, the very singing of the psalms and other sacred texts from the Scriptures imbued the monks with a deep sense of the value of God's creation. As Sister Joan Chittister put it in her essay *Monasticism: An Ancient Answer to Modern Problems*:

It is precisely this monastic sense of praise, humility, stewardship,

126

manual labour and community that taught Europe and made Europe fruitful and saved Western civilization. It is those things that we now, to our peril, have lost sight of.[6]

The Franciscan approach envisages a kind of natural 'brotherhood' of man with creation, which is neither pantheistic nor overly intellectual, but rather concrete. For example, St. Francis speaks of brother sun, sister moon and even sister death. This perception is not in contradiction with the more active approach to creation found in the Benedictine tradition, but rather complements it. In fact it was the Middle Ages, permeated by the living Catholic faith in God who created the world *ex nihilo* and *cum tempore*, which was the matrix of modern science.[7] However, after the Middle Ages, the intimate relation between faith and science was broken down, and this fragmentation was to be exemplified in the thought of the Enlightenment. The autonomy of science was exaggerated to such an extent that scientists no longer drew upon the moral truths propounded by the Church in order to evaluate rightly the technological applications of science. It is precisely this lack of moral consciousness within society that is at the root of current environmental problems.

In the Christian vision, God was absolutely free in creating the cosmos, which therefore could have been otherwise in any number of possible forms; the cosmos is thus contingent upon God's will. The universe, as its name implies, is a unity and is also unique. It is essentially good and rational. God is distinct from His creation and so pantheism in its various forms is to be excluded. However, in almost all non-Christian approaches to creation, there is at least a touch of pantheism which features heavily in many secular Green ideologies. Most Christian ecology books contain a consideration of the fact that Genesis 1:28 ('God blessed them, saying to them, "Be fruitful, multiply, fill the earth and conquer it. Be masters of the fish of the sea, the birds of heaven and all living animals on the earth"') must be viewed in relation to Genesis 2:15 ('The Lord God took the man and settled him in the garden of Eden to cultivate and take care of it.') In this way, man can never be regarded as having absolute sovereignty over creation, but rather a responsible stewardship, in which he is accountable to God the Creator. Human activity must be seen as a participation in the divine work of Creation following God's laws, whether natural or revealed.

127

The Apex of Creation

We see from the Old Testament that the subhuman world reaches its full significance only in relation to man and woman. On six occasions in the first chapter of Genesis it is stated that God sees as good that which He has created (Gen.1:4,10,12,18,21,25). However, after the creation of man and woman, it is stated that 'God saw all He had made, and indeed it was very good' (Gen.1:31). Creation only becomes very good, instead of merely good, after the creation of the human person, after man and woman are created as the apex of all God made, creatures endowed with intellect and free will. Moreover man and woman only find their full significance in relation to God in Christ. This is beautifully expressed in the poetry of Gerard Manley Hopkins:

> I am all at once what Christ is, since He was what I am, and
> This Jack, joke, poor potsherd, patch, matchwood, immortal diamond,
> Is immortal diamond.[8]

The Distraction of Feminism

Often, in current ecological thought, the relation of man and woman is distorted. In certain forms of feminism woman is seen as having been the subject of oppression for long periods of history, or is regarded as being in continual struggle with man in a Marxist perspective. Sometimes there is a desire for a superficial equality with man in terms of identity of gender, which has led to the errors of the so-called 'unisex' culture. These notions are far from the Christian vision in which woman and man are equal co-heirs with Christ but different in their biological and psychological constitution. Such differences between man and woman enrich the creation and the full theological consequences of these differences need to be further explored. Furthermore, the true role of woman in society and in the Church still requires further development. However the authentic liberation of woman and of man is that of a liberation from sin so as to be free in Christ.

Animal Rights and Human Wrongs

There is an essential distinction between man and the animals, a fact which is ignored by many ecologists among whom there is a tendency to regard animals as having the same dignity as human beings. Often one notes more concern for animal rights than for the rights of the unborn, as has been seen earlier in this book. In certain countries there are special cemeteries for dogs (I have seen one which is over one hundred years old) while the starving people of the Third World are often not properly buried. Certainly cruelty to animals is to be rejected. Often a person who is cruel to animals will also show little regard for his fellow human beings. With regard to man's treatment of animals, the Catechism of the Catholic Church states:

> Animals are God's creatures. He surrounds them with His providential care. By their mere existence they bless Him and give Him glory. Thus men owe them kindness. We should recall the gentleness with which saints like St. Francis of Assisi or St. Philip Neri treated animals … It is contrary to human dignity to cause animals to suffer or die needlessly. It is likewise unworthy to spend money on them that should as a priority go to the relief of human misery. One can love animals; one should not direct to them the affection due only to persons.[9]

Christ is the Key

The true nature of man and woman within the cosmos is revealed in the mystery of Christ, who as well as revealing the Most Holy Trinity also reveals perfect humanity. Indeed Christ is the Key who reveals the true meaning of creation. Such a Christocentric perspective is already found in certain of the Pauline letters (Col.1:15-20; Eph.1:3-14). This vision has been developed down the centuries by such theologians as St. Irenaeus and Blessed Duns Scotus. More recently Stanley Jaki has shown how the doctrine of the Incarnation safeguards the notion of creation. The expression 'only-begotten Son' is a powerful barrier against taking the world for another begetting or emanation of the divine.[10] The cosmos is also contingent as a divine choice among an infinite number of possible universes. The Incarnation of the Word closes the door upon any type of pantheism or deism, errors which appear in various ecological ideologies. Another contribution of orthodox, dogmatic Christianity is a very strong appreciation of time as actually experienced. That the Incarnation took place at a fixed point of time, marked by the invariable references to Pontius Pilate in all credal formulas, could but enhance the perception of the uniqueness of each moment and therefore of history. Since such uniqueness is inconceivable within the recurrence of cyclic ages, the Incarnation added further emphasis to a linear perception of time, which had been an integral part of Old Testament salvation history.[11] The full rationality of the cosmos is 'rooted in the belief in the strict divinity of the Logos'.[12] There is in fact a most specifically Christian theology of creation which alone can be the key to facing the present ecological crisis, as well as other moral problems.

Sin and the Environment

Catholic teaching has always affirmed that the beginnings of human history were marked with tragedy. G.K. Chesterton remarked that original sin is the most self-evident of all Christian dogmas.[13] The results of this have been described since biblical times. As the prophet Jeremiah says:

> How long will the land be in mourning, and the grass wither over all the countryside? The animals and birds are dying as a result of the wickedness of the inhabitants. For they say, 'God does not see our behaviour'.
>
> Jer. 12:4

Violence has been introduced into the cosmos as a result of original sin. In a certain sense the flood (Gen.6:5-9,17) represents an ecological punishment inflicted by God for man's sin, and the rainbow was the sign of God's covenant with Noah thereafter. Sin alienates us from God in the first place and also from our fellow human beings, from ourselves and from the natural world. It should be recalled that traditionally man is tempted in essentially three ways: the world, the flesh and the devil. Each of these exerts an evil influence on man inducing him to make a destructive use of God's creation, no longer for the glory of the Creator but for man's own selfish and perverted ends. In this context the existence of the devil is clear as the cosmic vandal.

Sin has thus had secondary effects on the cosmos which is worse off after the Fall. An echo of this is felt even in the material creation apart from man: 'It was not for any fault on the part of the creation that it was made unable to attain its purpose, it was made so by God' (Rom.8:20). Hence, in a certain sense, the whole cosmos needs to be recapitulated in Christ (Eph.1:10) in order to be freed 'from its slavery to decadence, to enjoy the same freedom and glory as the children of God' (Rom.8:21). This liberation occurs in the Redemption which is actualized through the Church.

Consideration of Christ's redemptive act should leave us in no doubt as to the fact that a healing of the relation of man to his environment is not a work which can be brought about solely by human hands. Since the damage caused to nature is essentially a moral problem and results from sin, Christ's Redemption needs to be applied. This approach is in sharp contrast to the heavily political and ideological notion of man as a self-sufficient being which is to be found in most secular ecologies of today. Christian ecology deals with God healing the cosmos through human instruments. The Cross is the tree of life, the victory of Christ over death and hence over the sinful use which men and women make of their environment. Only by applying the power of Christ crucified and risen can we re-establish peace within nature. The Paschal Mystery is, however, made present through the ministry of the Church in every age and every place.

From the New Testament the cosmic role of the Church can already be seen: 'He has put all things under His feet, and made Him, as the ruler of everything, the head of the Church; which is His body, the fullness of Him who fills the whole creation' (Eph.1:22). St. Paul also states in his letter to the Colossians:

> Before anything was created, He existed,
> and He holds all things in unity.
> Now the Church is His body,
> He is its head'
>
> Col.1:17-18

The Christian, exercising his kingly role, is a mediator of this redemption to the cosmos. The Church in her prayer and sacraments applies the power of Christ crucified and risen so as to restore peace to nature. Thus spirituality can never regard creation as isolated from the reality of Original Sin and the Redemption wrought by the Incarnation and the Paschal Mystery.

The End of the World

Finally, we know from the assurance of Christ Himself that the world, which had a beginning, will also have an end. However, such a consummation will not be brought about by human action. The pessimistic idea that the ecological crisis could provoke the end of the world seems to rob from God's hands domination over this final point in history. The final consummation of the cosmos, like its creation, is an action of God who is transcendent as well as immanent. Nevertheless the material cosmos is important because Christ has partaken of it and used it in His sacramental order. There will thus be a continuity between the cosmos of here and now and the new heavens and new earth (Rev.21:1).

In the words of Pope John Paul II, the way forward in an ecological formation 'must not be based on a rejection of the modern world or a vague desire to return to some "paradise lost"'.[14] Rather, what is needed to face the current problems in the environment is a clear presentation and proclamation of the Christian truths concerning Creator and Creation. This area provides a fertile field for ecumenical collaboration, since many churches and ecclesial communities have attempted to face the issue of the environment.[15] It is only in this context that we will be able to arrive in some fashion, but without any utopian ideology, at the vision which Isaiah proposes concerning a redeemed cosmos:

> The wolf lives with the lamb,
> the panther lies down with the kid,
> calf and lion cub feed together
> with a little boy to lead them.
> The cow and the bear make friends,
> their young lie down together.
> The lion eats straw like the ox.
> The infant plays over the cobra's hole;
> into the viper's lair
> the young child puts his hand.
> They do no hurt, no harm,

on all my holy mountain,
for the country is filled with the knowledge of the Lord
as the waters swell the sea.

Isaiah 11:6-9

NOTES

1. Pope John Paul II, *Peace with God the Creator, Peace with all of Creation*, Message for World Day of Peace (1990) 7.3.
2. Pope John Paul II, Encyclical Letter *Centesimus Annus*, 38.
3. See E. Holloway, *Catholicism: A New Synthesis*, Wallington, Surrey: Faith-Keyway (1976) pp. 105-14.
4. See Pope John Paul II, *Message for World Day of Peace* (1990) 6,7,15.1.
5. See Episcopal Conference of Lombardy, *La questione ambientale: aspetti etico-religiosi*, Milano: Centro Ambrosiano di Documentazione e Studi Religiosi (1988) pp.13-14.
6. Sister J. Chittister OSB, 'Monasticism: An Ancient Answer to Modern Problems' in E. Breuilly and M. Palmer (eds.) *Christianity and Ecology*, London: Cassell (1992) p. 73.
7. See S.L. Jaki, *The Road of Science and the Ways to God*, Edinburgh: Scottish Academic Press (1978) and idem. *The Savior of Science*, Washington: Regnery Gateway (1988).
8. G. M. Hopkins, 'That Nature is a Heraclitean Fire and of the Comfort of the Resurrection'.
9. *Catechism of the Catholic Church*, London: Geoffrey Chapman (1994) paragraphs 2416 and 2418, pp. 516-7.
10. See S.L. Jaki, *The Savior of Science*, Washington: Regnery Gateway (1988) pp. 72-3.
11. This argument is more fully developed in P. Haffner, *Creation and Scientific Creativity; A Study in the Thought of S.L. Jaki*, Front Royal: Christendom Press (1991) chapters 4 and 7.
12. S. L. Jaki, *The Savior of Science*, op.cit., p. 77.
13. G. K. Chesterton, *Orthodoxy*, New York: Image Books (1959) p. 15.
14. Pope John Paul II, Message for World Day of Peace (1990) 13.2.
15. See, for example, the Ecumenical Directory of the Pontifical Council for Promoting Christian Unity, n. 215. See also V. Guroian 'Toward Ecology as an Ecclesial Event; Orthodox Theology and Ecological Ethics' in *Communio* 18/1 (Spring 1991) pp. 89-110.

Science Facts

1. Global Warming

Global warming is the mother of all environmental scares. It is the linchpin of the radical Green agenda for dismantling the industrial model of society, reducing world population and returning to a simpler lifestyle. It is also the Achilles' heel of the Green movement as the gap between the doomsday scenario and the data is wider than that for any other Green scare.

The popular version tells us that the temperature of the atmosphere is rising owing to the discharge of certain greenhouse gases as the result of human activities, like burning solid fuels in power stations, driving cars and even growing rice. A rise in the global temperature of several degrees by the middle of the next century is predicted, accompanied by the melting of the polar ice caps, the spreading of deserts, the disruption of agriculture and other unpleasant consequences.

The first thing to say is that there is a greenhouse effect. As the surface of the earth is warmed by the sun it emits infrared radiation, some of which is 'trapped' by the blanket of greenhouse gases — carbon dioxide (CO_2), methane, hydrocarbons, water vapour and some others — which is an essential precondition for the survival of life on earth. Without this greenhouse effect, earth would be as lifeless as Mars or Venus, boiling hot during the day and freezing cold at night.

The second point, on which there is no disagreement, is that there has been a build-up of the greenhouse gases over the last century. CO_2 levels have risen by about 20 percent over the last century, from 293 parts per million (ppm) in 1888 to 351 ppm in 1988. Climatologist Robert Balling has calculated the increase in total greenhouse gases at what he called equivalent CO_2 levels as rising from 310 parts per million (ppm) in 1900 to nearly 440 ppm in 1990 — a rise of about 40 percent.[1]

The global warming argument is based on the assumption that human activities have effectively altered the composition of the atmosphere by pumping up the proportion of these greenhouse gases, thus trapping more radiation and causing warming. Over the last hundred years there has indeed been a warming in the global climate of about one half of a degree centigrade. However, as Balling has shown, not all of this rise can be accounted for by the increase of greenhouse gases. Much depends on where the measurements are taken since, owing to what is called the 'urban heat island effect', towns are hotter than the surrounding countryside. Also, it has been found that areas of desert, caused for example by overgrazing, can also affect temperatures, and that some allowances must be made for changes in the methods used to measure temperature over the last century. This means that the true extent of the warming is probably less than half a degree centigrade.

The problem — from the point of view of the alarmists — is that the warming, such as it is, has not been consistent. Nearly 70 percent of the warming took place in the first part of the period, before the majority of the human-generated greenhouse gases were produced in the great and exponential burst of industrial growth which followed World War II. This naturally puts a question mark over the extent to which changes in climate are really generated by human industrial activities. This was followed by a period of cooling from the 1940s to the 1970s, and it is worth remembering that the big climate scare of the mid-1970s was the New Ice Age, with scientists predicting that the glaciers were about to move South again. We then had some very hot years in the 1980s, and it was the record-breaking summers of some of those years which fuelled fears of catastrophic warming.

However, we now have data which puts those hot summers into perspective. Since 1979 satellite data has been collected which allows us to measure changes in atmospheric temperature much more accurately, by avoiding the urban heat island effect and other distorting factors. The data for the period 1979-94 show that in spite of some very hot years — including some of the hottest on record — there was a slight *cooling* over the period of 0.13°C.[2]

Therefore, although we can all agree that there have been changes in the composition of the atmosphere, including a significant build-up of greenhouse gases, there has been no corresponding global warming. The link between industrial activities and climate change becomes even weaker when we consider that the volume of greenhouse gas emissions which are anthropogenic (generated by man) pales into insignificance compared with emissions from natural sources over which we have no control. According to Dixy Lee Ray and Lou Guzzo:

> The largest source of greenhouse gas may well be termites, whose digestive activities are responsible for about 50 billion tons of CO_2 and methane annually. This is 10 times more than the present world production of CO_2 from burning fossil fuel.[3]

Another major natural source of greenhouse gases is volcanic eruption, and we appear to be living through a period of high volcanic activity.

> Some estimates from large volcanic eruptions in the past suggest that all of the air polluting materials produced by man since the beginning of the industrial revolution do not begin to equal the quantities of toxic materials, aerosols and particulates spewed into the air from just three volcanoes: Krakatoa in Indonesia in 1883, Mount Katmai in Alaska in 1912, and Hekla in Iceland in 1947. Despite these prodigious emissions, Krakatoa, for example, produced some chilly winters, spectacular sunsets, and a global temperature drop of 0.3 degrees Centigrade, but no climate change.[4]

There are big gaps in our understanding of influences on climate. We do not really understand the extent to which ocean currents and cloud cover affect climate. Any computer models which we create to predict the future will, therefore, be highly unreliable given the present state of uncertainty. In *The Heated Debate* Robert Balling tests the reliability of these models by comparing their predicted effects of a doubling of CO_2 some time in the next century with the observed consequences of an *actual* increase of 40 percent in CO_2 equivalent in the last century. As we have *already* experienced nearly half of the doubling of greenhouse gases in the atmosphere for which the doomsayers are predicting such dire consequences in the next century, and there have been no catastrophic or dramatic changes in climate over the period, the doomsday scenario becomes increasingly absurd. The climate modellers are unrepentant, however. Dr. Chris Folland of the UK Meteorological Office believes that:

... the data don't matter ... Besides we [the UN] are not basing our recommendations upon the data; we're basing them upon the climate models.[5]

Alarmists are thus reduced to looking at each other's computers instead of looking out of the window!

Another major influence on climate over which we have no control is the activity of sunspots, or magnetic storms on the surface of the sun. Dixy Lee Ray cites research by Dr. John Eddy of the National Centre for Atmospheric Research in the USA which indicates that periods characterised by high levels of sunspot activity correspond to warm spells on earth, and vice versa. For example, a virtual absence of sunspot activity between 1645 and 1715 corresponded with the late seventeenth century's 'Little Ice Age' when the Thames froze over and trees in the West of England exploded from the buildup in internal ice.[6]

Dr. Eddy's theory was supported by a paper presented to the European and National Astronomy Meeting in Edinburgh in April 1994 by Dr. John Butler, which drew on climate records held at the Armagh Observatory in Northern Ireland. These records began in 1795, and are therefore not quite the longest series in the world, as the records at Kew Gardens date from the 1770s. However they are not affected by the 'urban heat island' effect to the same extent as the Kew records, as Armagh has not grown on a par with London in the last two centuries. (Kew is now part of Greater London.) Analysis of the Armagh data showed that changes in climate are closely correlated with the length of sunspot cycles. These cycles have been abnormally short for the last 20 years, corresponding with a warming of climate. On the other hand, abnormally long sunspot cycles in the seventeenth century corresponded with the Little Ice Age. The case for human (anthropogenic) influences on the climate becomes weaker.

There is a mistaken view that most scientists agree that global warming is taking place, and that only a few 'mavericks' oppose the theory. In fact, amongst climatologists and other scientists directly involved in the issue, almost the reverse is true. A Gallup Poll of members of the American Geophysical Union and the American Meteorological Society taken in February 1992 found that only 18 percent thought that some global warming had occurred. 33 percent thought that there was not enough evidence to say, while 49 percent believed that there had been no warming — a majority of 82 percent against the view that global warming can be shown to be occurring. A letter signed by over 50 leading members of the American Meteorological Society warned, prior to the Rio de Janeiro Earth Summit, that policy initiatives which were being promoted by environmental groups:

> ... derive from highly uncertain scientific theories. They are based on the unsupported assumption that catastrophic global warming follows from the burning of fossil fuel and requires immediate action. We do not agree.[7]

As Joseph Bast and his fellow authors point out in *Eco-sanity*:

> Fifty scientists may seem to be a small number, but there are only about sixty climatologists in the U.S. who work with climate histories or global climate models.[8]

Even the media hype of global warming has been dying down. As Bast and his colleagues point out, in 1989 *Time* magazine replaced its 'Man of the Year' feature with the nomination of Earth as 'Planet of the Year', in recognition of the threat of global warming. By January 1994 *Time* was running an article called *The Ice Age Cometh?* and warning readers that talk about global warming had been 'apocalyptic' and to 'start worrying about the next ice age instead'.[9] Such are the vagaries of media fads. However the drive for policies based on global warming continues unabated at national and international levels. These policies would reduce the standard of living of both the rich and the poor countries if they were implemented. As long as they are based on unsubstantiated theories they should be resisted.

2. The Hole In The Ozone Layer

After global warming, the supposed thinning of the ozone layer as a result of the use of chlorofluorocarbons (CFCs) by man is probably the best known of the Green scares. The science of the ozone hole is less shaky than that behind global warming, although there are still important areas of disagreement. However, whereas there have as yet been no major public policy decisions based on global warming, CFCs have been banned as of 2000 under the Montreal Convention, and unilaterally in the USA as of 1995.

CFCs were invented in the 1930s and have provided us with the means of having cheap, safe refrigeration ever since. Their main application has been in food storage and transportation and in air conditioning systems. It is owing to CFCs that we now take it for granted that we can afford to eat food which is grown on the other side of the world. Not only do they give us a more interesting diet, they allow the people of less developed countries to participate in the world economy by finding a market for their produce, as well as preserving their own food from decay. CFCs also play a vital part in the safe storage of medicines in hot climates.

The theory is that these CFCs, when released into the atmosphere, climb into the stratosphere where they interact with ozone molecules by releasing their chlorine. This is alleged to lead to a thinning of the ozone, which normally screens out a proportion of the sun's ultraviolet rays. The increase in ultraviolet light reaching the earth is then supposed to lead to a greater incidence of skin cancer.

As a number of commentators have now pointed out, the evidence is questionable for every part of the scenario. First of all, ozone has only been measured since 1956 when Gordon Dobson, a British scientist, devised the unit which was called after him. Even given this short time span for measurement, we know that there are large natural fluctuations in ozone, by as much as 40 or 50 percent in some areas. Ozone levels rose during the 1960s and early 1970s, then fell during the 1980s, but who is to say what the 'normal' level should be? According to environmental scientist Fred Singer of the University of Virginia, these natural fluctuations are 'hundreds of times larger than the alleged steady change'.[10] Claims that ozone levels have dropped by two percent or five percent are thus not necessarily anything to worry about.

Even more to the point, scientists at the Belgian Meteorological Institute have shown that ozone measurements may have been inaccurate owing to a tendency to read decreases in sulphur dioxide (which has been falling as a result of pollution controls) as decreases in ozone. When this is factored out of the figures, there may have been a slight increase in ozone over the period of the feared decrease.[11]

It was Sir Gordon Dobson who first recorded the seasonal thinning of ozone over Antarctica (there is no 'hole') in 1956 and 1957, which he concluded was a natural phenomenon. The thinning was also described by two French scientists, P. Rigaud and B. Leroy, in 1958 who concluded that 'the thinning [is] related to the Polar Vortex and the recovery is sharp and complete'. In the light of claims from ozone scaremongers that the 'hole' dates from the announcement by the British Antarctic Survey in 1985, Rigaud and Leroy reviewed and republished their data in 1990.[12] The significance of these findings is that the thinning *could not have been caused by CFCs* since, although they were in use in the 1950s, their application was too limited to have been responsible for the phenomenon.

The link between the release of the man-made CFCs and the fluctuations in the ozone level is therefore questionable.

This is not to say that CFCs cannot react with ozone, but we have to keep it in perspective. The fact that man made chemical compounds are found in the stratosphere does not necessarily mean that a disaster is imminent. As Andrew Kenny put in an article for *The Spectator*:

> If you put urine at body temperature into a bucket of seawater at ambient temperature, there certainly will be a warming of the seawater. But it does not follow that if you pee into the ocean you will melt the polar ice caps.[13]

Kenny pointed out that there is a fatal flaw in the whole CFC/ozone hole theory: it fails its own critical empirical test. The scare is based on the claim that the destruction of the ozone layer by CFCs will allow more of the sun's ultraviolet light to reach the earth, thus causing an increase in skin cancers. However, there has been no increase in UV light measured at the earth's surface: on the contrary, *there has been a decrease*.[14] The National Cancer Institute in the USA used measurements taken across America between 1974-79 and 1980-85 to show that there had been a *decrease* in ultraviolet B (UVB) of 0.7 percent per year, on average.[15] Other studies from around the world have confirmed this trend. Only one study, published in *Science* in 1993, has indicated an increase in UV. This claimed an increase of UVB in Canada of 35 percent per year for the last four years.[16] However the paper was denounced by other scientists who demanded that *Science* print a retraction, as the claim was based on only four readings out of a total of over 300, and all of the four were taken in March 1993 when extraordinary weather conditions prevailed as a result of the deepest surface cyclone recorded over the northeastern United

States. After eliminating these four readings the trend was essentially zero.[17] Although *Science* would not retract the article they published a Technical Comment making the point that 'large, temporary UV variations are not unusual and do not indicate a trend'.[18]

The inconvenient fact that there is no measurable increase in UV light at the earth's surface has not prevented the alarmists from claiming that ozone depletion is responsible for the recent increase in skin cancers. Whilst it is true that some skin cancers are the result of exposure to increased UV, the risk of contracting them has more to do with where people live and the length of time they spend in the sun than with anything which is happening in the stratosphere. UV exposure becomes more intense the closer you get to the equator, increasing by one percent for every six miles south. Owing to increasing wealth and mobility, more people are able to travel to sunny climates for their holidays where they bake themselves in the sun. Inbetween times they top up the tan with UV lamps. There may well be other factors behind the increase in skin cancer, but the 'hole in the ozone layer' is unlikely to be one of them.

In spite of the fact that, as Andrew Kenny points out, the evidence linking CFCs with ozone depletion is about as convincing as the evidence linking Jews with the Black Death in the Middle Ages, the Greens scored a major victory on this battlefield. In 1987, 59 nations signed what became known as the Montreal Protocol, agreeing to half production of CFCs by the year 2000. Not satisfied with this, they renegotiated the protocol in 1990 to end production altogether by the end of the century.

Even this did not go far enough for Green extremists. In what must be regarded as one of the most blatant manipulations of science for political ends ever seen, the US National Aeronautics and Space Administration issued a press release in February 1992 warning that an ozone hole was about to open up over North America, bombarding US citizens with ultraviolet light. As a direct result, the US Senate passed an amendment requiring that CFCs be banned from 1995. In fact no 'hole' ever appeared in the ozone over the Northern hemisphere, and NASA acknowledged its mistake in April 1992. We are nevertheless left with the consequences.

The reason that CFCs became so widely used is that they were almost perfect for the job required. They were stable and cheap. They replaced other refrigerants, like ammonia and sulphur dioxide, which

141

were dangerous and toxic. They were also coming to the end of their patents, which would have made them even cheaper. There are, as yet, no suitable substitutes. All of the alternatives are much more expensive as well as more volatile. They are not compatible with each other, and yet we will soon have to start replacing all refrigeration and air conditioning systems without having a generally recognised suitable alternative to CFCs. Few people have even begun to comprehend the costs. First, the banning of CFCs and the inevitable rise in all refrigeration costs will not only lower the standard of living but will almost certainly lead to more deaths from preventable diseases in the developing countries. This is unlikely to worry the middle class white élites who run the Green movement since, as Andrew Kenny points out:

> The outstanding feature of the Greens is that they are rich. The outstanding feature of their victims is that they are poor.[19]

The cash costs to the developed nations are so staggering as to be difficult to take in. In a paper for the Competitive Enterprise Institute entitled *The High Cost of Cool* Ben Lieberman estimated the costs to the US economy of banning CFCs as amounting to something between 44 and 99 *billion* dollars. This takes into account the replacement or refurbishment of vehicle air conditioners, domestic and commercial refrigeration and other uses. Lieberman describes the CFC ban, without overstatement, as 'likely [to] become the single most expensive environmental measure taken to date'.[20] Other countries will face similar costs, although the USA will be particularly hard hit owing to its widespread dependence on air conditioning. These costs will not be absorbed by the wicked capitalist entrepreneurs of Green mythology: they will be directly reflected in everyone's cost of living expenses.

In *Environmental Overkill* Dixy Lee Ray and Lou Guzzo quote from an extraordinarily frank account by Richard Benedick, the US negotiator for the Montreal Protocol, of the way in which the treaty was drawn up. He writes:

> Perhaps the most extraordinary aspect of the treaty was its imposition of short term economic costs to protect human health and the environment against unproved future dangers ... dangers that rested on scien-

tific theories, rather than on firm data. At the time of the negotiations and signing, no measurable evidence of damage existed.[21]

There is still none. Benedick goes on:

> By their action the signatory countries sounded the death knell for an important part of the international chemical industry ... the negotiators established target dates for replacing products that had become synonymous with modern standards of living, even though the requisite technologies did not yet exist.[22]

When the bills for the Montreal Protocol start to come in, it is just possible that the public may become less enthusiastic about what the Greens refer to as The Precautionary Principle, which might also be termed the Let's-Pass-the-Law-Now-Without-Waiting-for-the-Evidence approach to public policy.

3. Species Extinction

Claims that species are becoming extinct at an alarming rate are a staple of Green fundraising. *How many species have to disappear before you join us?* and *By the time you finish reading this advertisement XX species will have become extinct* are familiar slogans. In fact we have no idea of how many species there are, and how many of them (if any) are currently vanishing into the black hole of extinction.

The World Wide Fund for Nature (WWF) produced a pamphlet called *Biological Diversity* which, in different paragraphs, gave estimates of the total number of species ranging between 5 million and 100 million. In the absence of anything approaching a reasonable approximation of the total number of species, the frequently made claims that, by such and such a year, 25 percent or 50 percent of all species will have disappeared, is meaningless. It is impossible to calculate a fraction of an unknown total, even if we knew how many species were becoming extinct in absolute terms. But we don't.

In 1990 the Rotary Club of Great Britain entered into a partnership with Marie Stopes International (MSI) to raise funds for population control projects. Members received packs of information making alarming claims about the consequences of population growth, including the statement that 'overpopulation is responsible for ... the loss of 5,000 species a year'. Another sheet in the same pack gave the rate of extinction as 500 species per day. The second rate is 36 times greater than the first, so clearly they could not both be correct.

A Rotarian decided to challenge these claims by requesting a list of the thousands of species which must have become extinct in recent years. He was told that no such list existed, but he received from MSI a list of species *thought to have become extinct* in the decade of the 1980s. There were four. Only one, the Atitlan Giant Grebe, was declared definitely extinct. The other three — a giant earwig, a macaw and a boa constrictor — had not been seen for some years. However, it is quite common for species to be declared extinct and then turn up unexpectedly. For example, the Noisy Shout Bird of Western Australia had been 'extinct' for several years before it was found a few miles outside Perth.

So, from this list of four species thought to have become extinct in a decade, MSI had extrapolated a rate of 500 extinctions per day. Such is the respect for scientific accuracy amongst the Greens.

Julian Simon, of the University of Maryland, has done more work to expose what he calls the 'statistical flummery about species loss' than anyone else. He has traced the outlandish claims back to a book called *The Sinking Ark* by Norman Myers, published in 1979.[23] Myers claimed that, between 1600 and 1900, species were becoming extinct at the rate of one every four years. Between 1900 and 1980 he put it at one a year, and then extrapolated from this to 40,000 per year for the rest of the century.

Partly as a result of the questions which were being raised about species extinction by Julian Simon, working first alone and then with Aaron Wildavsky, the International Union for the Conservation of Nature and Natural Resources (IUCN) commissioned a number of authors to write chapters for a book called *Tropical Deforestation and Species Extinction*.[24] As Simon has written:

> The results of that project must be considered amazing. All the authors are ecologists who express concern about the rate of extinction. Nevertheless, they all agree that the rate of *known* extinctions has been and continues to be very low.[25]

Simon then lists a number of quotes from different chapters in the book which back up his position:

Known extinction rates are very low (p.94) ... actual extinctions remain low ... many endangered species appear to have either an almost miraculous capacity for survival or a guardian angel is watching over their destiny! (p.102) ... The group of zoologists could not find a single known animal species which could properly be described as extinct, in spite of the massive reduction in area and fragmentation of their habitats (p.127) ... Closer examination of the existing data ... supports the affirmation that little or no species extinction has yet occurred (p.128).

Simon ends his long list of quotes with one from two contributors who admit that:

There are many reasons why recorded extinctions do not match the predictions and extrapolations that are frequently published (p.93).

Although they are too scholarly to mention this, the main reason is the desire on the part of environmental pressure groups to extract donations from well-meaning members of the public.

4. Deforestation

Contrary to popular belief, there is no shortage of trees in the world. The area of the earth's surface covered by forest has scarcely changed in 40 years. It represented 3.5 million hectares in 1949 and 4 million in 1988, according to figures from the Production Yearbooks of the United Nations Food and Agriculture Organisation. Although there is a considerable degree of speculation involved in compiling these figures, which would make it unwise to attach too much importance to year-on-year increases or decreases, it seems clear that there has been very little fluctuation in the earth's forest cover in the last part of this century.

However there have been dramatic changes within particular regions. Most of the world's industrial wood needs (nearly 75 per cent) are met from forests in the northern temperate zones, but forested areas in these northern industrial countries are increasing. As Roger Sedjo of the Washington-based organisation Resources for the Future has shown, although the United States is the world's number one timber producer, accounting for 25 percent of the world total, U.S. forests continue to expand.[26]

The principal reason for this has been the development of plantation forests, which can meet demands for wood in a much more efficient way than the taking of wood from natural sources. Sedjo compares the development of plantation forestry to the transition from hunting and gathering to farming as a means of obtaining food thousands of years ago.

Even in the tropics, the larger part of the wood harvested comes from plantations. India heads the list of tropical countries establishing forest plantations, adding 1.7 million hectares every year. Brazil comes next with 200,000 hectares a year.[27] Although the Brazilian plantations account for only 2 percent of its forests, they provide 60 per cent of the wood harvested.[28] According to Sedjo:

> The world's current industrial wood consumption requirements could be produced on about 200 million hectares of good forestland, an area only about 5 per cent of the world's current forestland ... Natural forests no longer serve as a major source of industrial wood.[29]

Nevertheless, there are parts of the world which have experienced rapid deforestation, in particular the tropical rain forests which are said the be home to the majority of the world's species. Rain forest loss is therefore supposed to correlate with species extinction.

The areas covered by the tropical forests are still vast, representing about 13 percent of the earth's land surface. Vast tracts of it are so sparsely populated, or unpopulated, that accurate data is hard to come by, and what there is can be controversial. The Amazon rain forest, which attracts most of the attention, covers 6.5 million square kilometres, of which 3.5 million is in Brazil. Brazil has created what is known as Legal Amazonia, which covers nearly 5 million square kilometres, or 57 per cent of Brazil's territory. The entire continent of Europe could fit inside Legal Amazonia, and 70 per cent of it is tropical forest. Dramatic claims have been made about the Amazonian forests being 'scraped from the face of the earth' by the beginning of the next century. However, Evaristo de Miranda, professor of ecology at Sao Paulo University and research coordinator of the Environmental Monitoring Center of the Brazilian Agriculture Ministry, has shown these to be exaggerated.[30]

In particular, he takes Vice President Al Gore to task for some of the wilder statements made in his book *Earth in the Balance* in which Gore claims, amongst other things, that 20 percent of the Amazonian rain forests have been lost in recent years, and that deforestation is continuing at the rate of over 80,000 square kilometres a year.

De Miranda uses satellite data collected by the National Institute for Space Research between 1978 and 1990 to show that deforestation could never have reached 80,000 square kilometres a year, having averaged 21,130 square kilometres throughout the 1980s. Expressed as a percentage of total forest lost per year, rates peaked between 1978-1988 at 0.54 percent a year. They fell to 0.30 percent in 1990-91, and are still falling. Whatever the problems in the Amazon, it will clearly be many lifetimes before the forests disappear, even if nothing happens to slow down the rate of clearance.

The clearance of rain forest has little to do with commercial logging, which makes the media-friendly protests outside high-class furniture stores irrelevant. It has more to do with the conversion of forestland for agriculture, and the reason for the peak in the late 1980s was a series of perverse incentives which the Brazilian government offered to peasants to clear forestland for agriculture, including tax credits, subsidies and cheap loans. These incentives encouraged excessive clearance and poor land management. Since they have been discontinued, rates of clearance have slowed.

However, the clearance of forest for farmland is not necessarily a bad thing. As Roger Sedjo points out:

> Countries that have achieved economic development almost always had an early period in which forestlands were rapidly converted to productive agricultural lands.[31]

In the days of Robin Hood Britain was covered with forests from end to end, but few people now would accept the standard of living of the Merrie Men. Similarly, the lifestyle of the rain forest Indian, weaving bodily adornments from leaves and living off nutritious bark and berries, probably holds more charm for white, middle class environmentalists than it does for the Indians.

According to the United Nations Food and Agriculture Organisation, between 1980 and 1990 tropical rain forest was being lost at the rate of 0.8 percent a year. The highest rates were sustained in Central America (1.5 percent) and Southeast Asia (1.6 percent), the lowest in

147

the Caribbean (0.3 percent) and Central Africa (0.5 percent).[32] It is true that some countries have experienced serious environmental damage through deforestation, usually as the direct result of misconceived political policies. However, the extravagant claims made by environmental groups, like the advertisement by Friends of the Earth in the UK claiming that 'the last of the rain forest hardwoods are being sold off,'[33] have more to do with fundraising than science.

NOTES

1. Robert Balling, 'Global Warming: Messy Models, Decent Data, and Pointless Policy' in Ronald Bailey (ed.) *The True State of the Planet*, New York: The Free Press, (1995) p. 87. For a more detailed exposition of the data by Balling see *The Heated Debate: Greenhouse Predictions versus Climate Reality*, San Francisco: Pacific Research Institute (1992).

2. Ibid., pp. 91 and 95-6.

3. Dixy Lee Ray with Lou Guzzo, *Trashing the Planet*, New York: Harper Collins (1992), p. 33.

4. Ibid., pp. 37-8.

5. Chris Folland, Presentation at Asheville, North Carolina, reported in Patrick Michaels, *Sound and Fury: The Science and Politics of Global Warming*, Washington DC: Cato Institute (1992) pp. 82-3, and quoted in Roger Bate and Julian Morris, *Global Warming: Apocalypse or Hot Air?* London: Institute of Economic Affairs (1994) p. 23.

6. John Eddy, 'C-14 Radioactivity in Tree Rings', *Access to Energy*, Vol 9 No 7 (1982); John Eddy, 'The Case of the Missing Sunspots', *Scientific American* (1977); cited in Dixy Lee Ray with Lou Guzzo, op.cit., pp. 39-41.

7. Gallup Poll and letter both quoted by Patrick Michaels, 'Conspiracy, Consensus or Correlation?', *World Climate Review* (Winter 1993) pp. 8-11.

8. Joseph L. Bast, Peter J. Hill, Richard C. Rue, *Eco-sanity: A Common Sense Guide to Environmentalism*, Lanham, Maryland: Madison Books (1994) pp. 55-6.

9. Joseph Bast *et al.*, op.cit, pp. 53 and 62. First *Time* story January 1989; second *Time* story 31 January 1994.

10. Fred Singer, 'My Adventures in the Ozone Hole', *National Review* (30 June 1989) p. 36; quoted in Ronald Bailey, *Ecoscam: The False Proph-*

ets of Ecological Apocalypse, New York: St Martin's Press (1993) p. 132.

11. Dirk de Muer and H. De Backer, 'Revision of 20 Years of Dobson Total Ozone Data at Uccle (Belgium); Fictitious Dobson Total Ozone Trends Induced by Sulphur Dioxide Trends', *Journal of Geophysical Research — Atmospheres* (20 April 1992) 5921; quoted in Ronald Bailey, op.cit., p. 132.

12. P. Rigaud and B. Leroy, 'Presumptive Evidence for a Low Value of the Total Ozone Content Above Antarctica in September 1958', *Annales Geophysicae* 8 (11)(1990) pp. 791-94. Quoted in Ron Bailey, *Ecoscam: The False Prophets of Ecological Apocalypse*, New York: St Martin's Press (1993) p. 135.

13. Andrew Kenny, 'The Earth Is Fine; The Problem is The Greens', *The Spectator* (12 March 1994) pp. 9-11.

14. Stuart A. Penkett, 'Ultraviolet Levels Down Not Up', *Nature*, Vol 3431 (28 September 1989) p.283; quoted in Dixy Lee Ray with Lou Guzzo, *Environmental Overkill: Whatever Happened to Common Sense?*, Washington: Regnery Gateway, (1993) p. 39.

15. Joseph Scotto, Gerald Cotton, Frederick Urback *et al*, 'Biologically Effective Ultraviolet Radiation: Surface Measurements in the United States, 1974-1985', *Science*, Vol 239 (12 February 1988) pp. 762-4; quoted in Dixy Lee Ray with Lou Guzzo, *Environmental Overkill*, op.cit., p. 39.

16. J. B. Kerr and C. T. McElroy, *Science*, Vol 262 (1993) p. 1032.

17. Adrian Berry, 'Laying the Ozone Scare', *The Sunday Telegraph* (5 March 1994) p. 16.

18. Patrick Michaels, S. Fred Singer and Paul C. Knappenberger, 'Analyzing Ultraviolet-B Radiation: Is There a Trend?', *Science*, Vol 264 (27 May 1994) pp. 1341-2.

19. Andrew Kenny, op.cit., p. 10.

20. Ben Lieberman, *The High Cost of Cool: The Economic Impact of the CFC Phaseout in the United States*, Washington: Competitive Enterprise Institute (June 1994) p. 14.

21. Richard E. Benedick, *Ozone Diplomacy*, Harvard University Press (1991) pp. 1-2; quoted in Dixy Lee Ray and Lou Guzzo, *Environmental Overkill*, op.cit., p. 46.

22. Ibid. pp.1-2.

23. Norman Myers, *The Sinking Ark*, New York: Pergamon Press (1979).

24. T.C. Whitemore and J.A. Sayer (eds.) *Tropical Deforestation and Spe-*

cies Extinction, Chapman and Hall (1992).

25. Julian L. Simon ,'Post Debate Statement', from Julian L. Simon and Norman Myers, *Scarcity or Abundance: A Debate on the Environment*, New York: W.W. Norton (1994) p. 200.

26. Roger Sedjo, 'Forests: Conflicting Signals' in Ron Bailey (ed.) *The True State of the Planet*, New York: The Free Press (1995) pp. 188-90.

27. Ibid., p. 196.

28. Ibid., p. 188.

29. Ibid., pp. 180 and 188.

30. Evaristo E. de Miranda, 'Tropical Rain Forests: Myths and Facts', in John A. Baden (ed.) *Environmental Gore: A Constructive Response to Earth in the Balance*, San Francisco: Pacific Research Institute (1994).

31. Roger Sedjo, op.cit., p, 204.

32. *Forest Resources Assessment 1990: Tropical Countries*, FAO Forestry Paper 112, Rome: United Nations Food and Agriculture Organisation (1993) p. 156.

33. Advertisement appearing in British papers in June 1988, with the headline 'How Many Rain forest Species Must Become Extinct Before You Join Us?'

Bibliography

Baden, J.A. (ed.) *Environmental Gore: A Constructive Response to "Earth in the Balance"*, San Francisco: Pacific Research Institute (1994).

Bailey, R., *Eco-Scam: The False Prophets of Ecological Apocalypse*, New York: St Martin's Press (1993).

Bailey, R. (ed.) *The True State of the Planet*, New York: The Free Press (1995).

Balling, R.C., *The Heated Debate: Greenhouse Predictions versus Climate Reality*, San Francisco: Pacific Research Institute (1992).

Bate, R. and Morris, J., *Global Warming: Apocalypse or Hot Air?*, London: Institute of Economic Affairs (1994).

Bernstam, M.S., *The Wealth of Nations and the Environment*, London: Institute of Economic Affairs (1991).

Fumento, M., *Science Under Siege: Balancing Technology and the Environment*, New York: William Morrow and Co. (1993).

Michaels, P., *Sound and Fury: The Science and Politics of Global Warming*, Washington DC: Cato Institute (1992).

Morris, J., *The Political Economy of Land Degradation: Pressure Groups, Foreign Aid and the Myth of Man-Made Deserts*, London: Institute of Economic Affairs, 1995.

Myers, N., and Simon, J.L., *Scarcity or Abundance? A Debate on the*

Environment, New York: W.W. Norton and Co (1994).

Ray, D.L. with Guzzo, L.R., *Environmental Overkill: Whatever Happened to Common Sense?* Washington DC: Regnery Gateway (1993).

Ray, D.L. with Guzzo L.R., *Trashing the Planet: How Science Can Help Us Deal with Acid Rain, Depletion of the Ozone and Nuclear Waste (Among Other Things)*, Washington DC: Regnery Gateway (1990).

Simon, J.L., *Population Matters: People, Resources, Environment and Immigration*, New Brunswick: Transaction Publishers (1990).

Simon, J.L., *The Ultimate Resource*, New Jersey: Princeton University Press (1981).

Simon, J.L. and Kahn, H., *The Resourceful Earth: A Response to 'Global 2000':* Oxford: Basil Blackwell (1984).

Sugg, I. and Kreuter, U., *Elephants and Ivory: Lessons from the Trade Ban*, London: Institute of Economic Affairs (1994).

't Sas-Rolfes, M., *Rhinos: Conservation, Economics and Trade-Offs*, London: Institute of Economic Affairs (1995).

Authors

Paul Haffner was born in London in 1954 and was educated at St. John's College, Southsea and Corpus Christi College, Oxford, where he read physics. After seminary studies at the Venerable English College and the Pontifical Gregorian University, Rome, he was ordained priest for the diocese of Portsmouth in 1981. From 1982 to 1984 Fr. Haffner was a curate in Aldershot. From 1984 to 1987 he was in Rome preparing his doctoral thesis which was published under the title *Faith in God the Creator in Relation to Modern Science According to the works of S.L. Jaki*. Between 1987-91 he was a lecturer at the Pontifical Gregorian University, the Pontifical Institute *Regina Mundi* and the Seminary of the Missionaries of the Faith in Rome, and worked part-time at the Pontifical Academy of Sciences. In 1991 his book *Creation and Scientific Creativity: A Study in the Thought of S.L. Jaki* was published. From 1992 to 1993 Fr. Haffner worked at the Pontifical Council for Promoting Christian Unity, and continued lecturing on science and theology at the Pontifical Gregorian University, Rome. From 1994 he has also been lecturing at the Pontifical Lateran University and the Athenaeum *Regina Apostolorum* of the Legionaries of Christ. His book *The Mystery of Creation* was published in 1995.

Joseph Kirwan was born in India in 1910, the son of a Rifle Brigade Sergeant Major. He was educated at St. Mary's Elementary School, Sunderland and Plater College, Oxford (the Catholic Workers' College). His MA degree course in Philosophy, Politics and Economics at St Catherine's College, Oxford was interrupted by wartime service with the infantry in Burma. He was tutor and bursar of Plater College from 1948-62 and Principal from 1962-77. He was a founder member of the executive of the European Union of Christian Democratic Workers, based in Brussels. He translated, with commentary, the encyclicals *Rerum Novarum, Mater et Magistra* and *Laborem Exercens*. He translated *The Church and Social Justice* by Calvez and Perrin, *Prayer as a Political Problem* by Danielou and *The Challenge of Hunger* by Drogat.

Robert Whelan was educated at the John Fisher School, Purley and Trinity College Cambridge, where he read English. He wrote and produced a series of educational videos for the Family Education Trust including *The Truth About AIDS*, *The Great Population Hoax*, *Facing Facts on Population* and *The Three R's of Family Life*. His publications include *Mounting Greenery, Broken Homes and Battered Children, Choices in Childbearing, Teaching Sex in Schools* and (with Roger Cummins) *Making a Lottery of Good Causes*. He has written articles on the environmental movement for *The Spectator, Economic Affairs* and other periodicals. He is Assistant Director of the Health and Welfare Unit of the Institute of Economic Affairs.

Index

155